Jochen Kerdels

Mastering OpenSCAD

within 10 projects

Bibliografische Information der Deutschen Nationalbibliothek:
Die Deutsche Nationalbibliothek verzeichnet diese Publikation in der Deutschen
Nationalbibliografie; detaillierte bibliografische Daten sind im Internet über
http://dnb.dnb.de abrufbar.

Herstellung und Verlag:
BoD — Books on Demand, Norderstedt

ISBN: 9783753458588

Contents

Introduction

OpenSCAD allows you to create three-dimensional models using **Constructive Solid Geometry** (CSG). The idea is to create complex geometries by combining a limited set of simple basic elements such as spheres, cylinders or boxes - a bit like how you used to play with building blocks as a child.

The special feature of OpenSCAD is that the geometry is specified via a purely textual description and not, for example, by using a pointing device in a graphical editor. This approach predestines OpenSCAD for a whole range of use cases that would be more difficult to implement in systems with a more interactive usage scheme. For example:

- fully parameterizable design of technical components,

- generation of geometries based on algorithms or mathematical descriptions,

- creation and use of geometry libraries,

- use in automated environments.

Of course, there are also use cases for which OpenSCAD is not suitable. These include, for example, the creation of artistic or photorealistic 3D graphics and animations. The unusual approach of describing geometry textually may initially give the impression that it is difficult and laborious to work in this way. Fortunately, this is not the case. The necessary learning curve is much flatter than it appears at first glance. Once you have internalized a few basic principles of this way of working, you can create even complex geometries without much difficulty. This book will help you to learn these basic principles quickly and easily by working through ten sample projects.

The projects are aimed in particular at those who want to design three-dimensional objects for their 3D printer or CNC milling machine. It is precisely in this area of application that OpenSCAD shines due to its high level of parameterizability.

1.1   Availability of OpenSCAD

OpenSCAD is a freely available, open source software that you can download for free from the website www.openscad.org. Versions for Windows, MacOS and Linux are offered in the download section of the website. This book refers to OpenSCAD version 2019.05.

Program Overview

Before we get into the basic functionality of OpenSCAD in the next chapter, let's first get an overview of the program's user interface and some of its standard functions and settings.

2.1 Start Screen

After starting OpenSCAD, you are greeted by a small startup window (Figure 2.1). The button *New* starts the program with an empty, not yet saved file. The *Open* button takes you to a file selection dialog where you can select and load an existing file. OpenSCAD files end with the file extension `.scad`. These are simple text files. The button *Help* opens an internet browser with the online help of the program. Below these three buttons there are two lists. The list on the left shows files recently edited with OpenSCAD. If you select one of these files, the *Open Recent* button below the list becomes active and clicking on this button will then open the corresponding file. Beware: you might be tempted to click the *Open* button above the list after selecting a file. This will not work as expected and will lead you back to the file selection dialog. The list on the right offers a number of thematically grouped examples. A small triangle is displayed in front

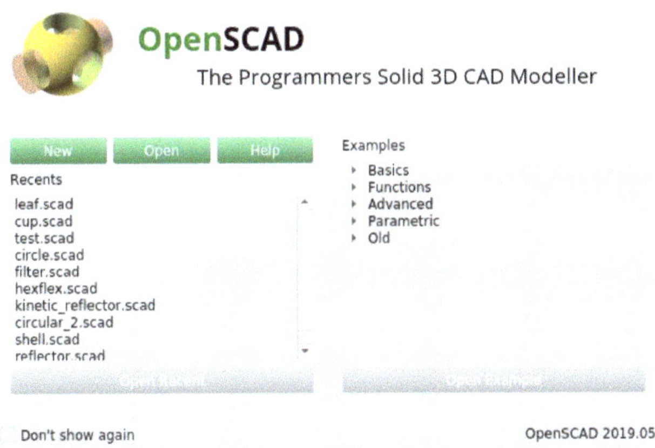

Figure 2.1: The start screen of OpenSCAD

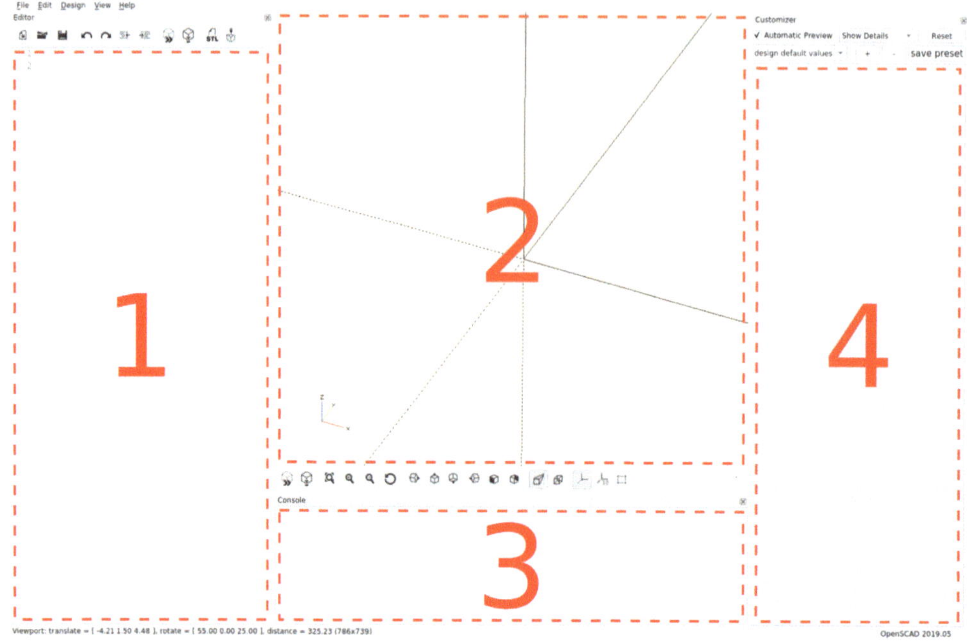

Figure 2.2: The user interface of OpenSCAD

of each topic. Clicking on the triangle "unfolds" the topic and you can select one of the example files. This activates the button *Open Example* below the list, with which one can open the selected example. Alternatively, in both lists you can open a selected file by double-clicking it. If you do not want to be greeted by this startup window every time you start OpenSCAD, you can disable it by checking the *Don't show again* checkbox at the bottom left.

For now, let's start OpenSCAD with a new, empty file (*New* button) and take a look at the program's user interface.

2.2   The User Interface

The user interface (Figure 2.2) is divided into **four areas**. The **first area** is located on the left side. This is a simple text editor, which is the main input interface for OpenSCAD. All modeling of geometries takes place here.

The **second area** is located in the center of the program window. This is an output window that provides a three-dimensional representation of the described geometries. The view can be changed by clicking and dragging with the mouse. If the left mouse button is held down, the display can be rotated. If the right mouse button is held down, the view is shifted. The mouse wheel can be used to zoom in and out of the view. Further adjustments of the display are available via the toolbar below the output window as well as via the menu item *View* in the program menu (top left). We will explore the exact details of these functions later during the sample projects.

The **third area** contains the console output of the program. It is located below the 3D output window. Here textual feedback of the program appears after or during certain actions are executed. The feedback helps, for example, to find errors in the geometry description or to recognize whether a calculation has been completed.

The **fourth area** is located on the right side of the program window. It is the *Customizer*. As the name suggests, this program area is used to configure or adapt the current model. OpenSCAD interprets certain global variables of the model as parameters and automatically generates a corresponding graphical user interface for them in which the parameters can be set. The resulting set of parameters can then be saved as a *preset* and reloaded at a later time. Experience shows that this window is only used for very specific applications. It is therefore only used occasionally.

The arrangement of the user interface into these four areas can be adjusted as needed. If you move the mouse to the border between two areas (Figure 2.3), you can move this border with the left mouse button held down. If you want to hide an area, you can do this by clicking on the framed small "x" in the upper right corner of the respective area. Alternatively, you can hide and show the individual areas with the menu entries *Hide editor*, *Hide console* and *Hide Customizer* located in the *View* program menu. If you want to change the relative position of an area within the user interface (e.g. move the text editor to the right side), click with the mouse on the upper part of that area (red shaded regions in figure 2.3) and move it with the left mouse button held down.

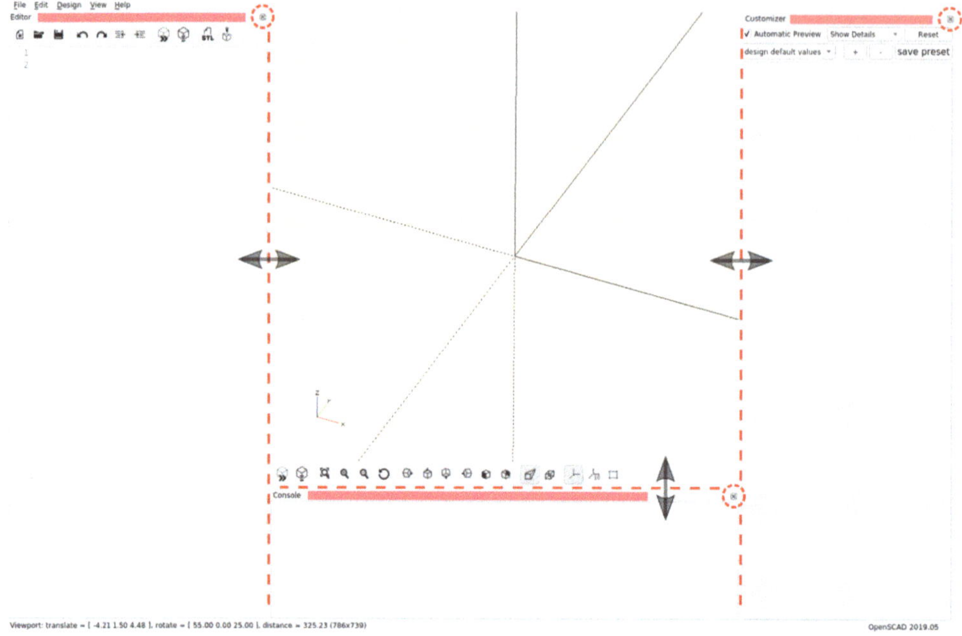

Figure 2.3: Adjustment of the different areas

2.3 The Program Menu

The program menu of OpenSCAD is quite similar to that of other programs. Therefore, we will only give a short overview at this point and will not go into specific functions until later.

As expected, the **File** menu contains functions for creating, opening, saving and closing model files. In addition, you have access to a list of recently used files, the export functions and the library directory of OpenSCAD.

The **Edit** menu provides a range of functions that relate to the text editor area. You can find typical functions like copy, paste or find and replace in this menu. Beyond these text functions you will also find the global settings of OpenSCAD here.

The **Design** menu contains two core functions of OpenSCAD, which we will use frequently: *Preview* and *Render*. The preview function creates a three-dimensional preview of the current geometry as quickly as possible and displays it in the output window. In most cases the result of this fast preview is without visible errors and supports the work immensely. However, the geometry created this way cannot be exported. For this, the second function, render, must be called. Rendering a complex geometry can take quite a while. Therefore, one usually only calls render if one wants to export the geometry or if the quick preview shows visible errors. Besides these two central functions, the checkbox *Automatic Reload and Preview* can also be found in the *Design* menu. If this feature is enabled, OpenSCAD observes the current geometry file. If the file has changed it is automatically reloaded and a quick preview is triggered. This feature turns out to be extremely handy during regular workflow: After making a change to the current geometry description in the text editor, it is common to save this change with the shortkey CTRL + S. As soon as you do this, the output window is automatically updated and you can immediately examine the results of the change. Without this automatic update, you would have to manually trigger a preview after each change. The *Automatic Reload and Preview* feature also allows you to use an external text editor instead of the internal one while still utilizing the output window of OpenSCAD in parallel.

The **View** menu has already been mentioned in the previous section. It offers numerous functions with which you can influence and configure the output window.

The last menu, **Help**, refers to various online resources that can support you in the use of OpenSCAD. Particularly noteworthy is the entry *Cheat Sheet*. It provides a very handy summary of all OpenSCAD commands and functions. Another very useful item is *Font List*. It provides an overview of the fonts available in OpenSCAD.

Since you operate OpenSCAD to a large extent with a keyboard rather than a mouse, it is worthwhile to learn the shortkeys of frequently used functions. You can find the shortkey of a function on the right side of the function's menu entry. Some of the functions are also accessible through icons on the program surface. If you hover the mouse pointer for a short moment over such an icon, a small explanation as well as the associated shortkey of the respective function will be shown.

OpenSCAD Basics

As mentioned before, geometric models in OpenSCAD are described by a textual description. At first glance, this description resembles a program written in a programming language such as Javascript or C. Especially if you have some programming experience, this apparent similarity can lead to some misunderstandings and misguided intuitions. Although the textual description reminds of classical program code, it is **not** a program. Rather, it is the *specification of a geometric structure*. In the course of the following sections, this difference will become more apparent. The focus of this chapter lies on conveying the essential concepts and functionality of OpenSCAD using select examples. An exhaustive description of all functions can be found at the end of the book as well as in the online documentation of OpenSCAD.

3.1 Basic Building Blocks

Let's start by describing our first geometry in OpenSCAD. If you have not already done so, now would be a good time to start OpenSCAD with an empty or new file. The OpenSCAD program window should show the internal editor, the output window and the console view. You can hide the Customizer for now.

The basis of any geometry in OpenSCAD are so-called *primitives*. These are two or three dimensional basic shapes that we can use as building blocks for our model. Let's create a simple sphere. To do this, enter the following into the editor:

```
sphere(10);
```

If you now run a preview (*F5*), the output window should show a sphere with a radius of 10 millimeters.

Also take a look at the console window. You should find a number of messages that were generated as part of the preview. The second to last line of this output should contain the message *Compile and preview finished*. (Figure 3.1).

If instead there is a red marked ERROR in the console output, something went wrong (Figure 3.2). Maybe you mistyped? Or maybe you forgot the semicolon at the end of

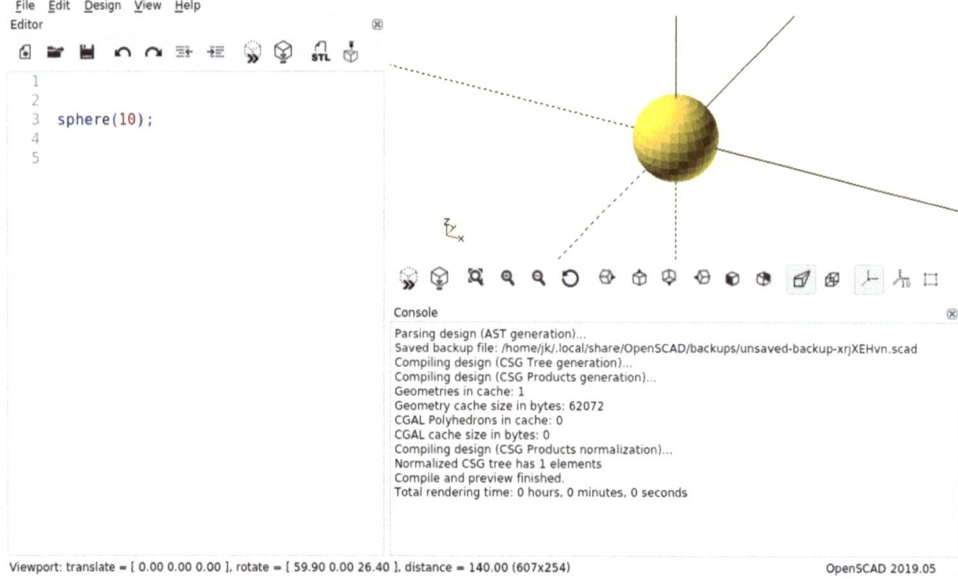

Figure 3.1: Successful rendering of the preview

the line? Did you perhaps write *sphere* with a capital *S* instead of a small one? Try to find the mistake and run the preview (*F5*) again.

Each basic shape in OpenSCAD has a unique name, which is always followed by a list of parameters in round brackets and a terminating semicolon. In the example above, the radius of the sphere is the first parameter. Each parameter also has a name and in general it is better to include this name. In the case of the sphere, the radius parameter has the name *r* and using this parameter name would look like this:

```
sphere(r = 10);
```

Even if it requires a bit more typing effort, using the parameter name has two advantages. First, the geometry description becomes more readable. Second, you don't have to remember the exact order of the parameters in case a basic shape has multiple ones. This is also the case with the sphere. Instead of the radius, you can also define a sphere by giving it a diameter:

```
sphere(d = 10);
```

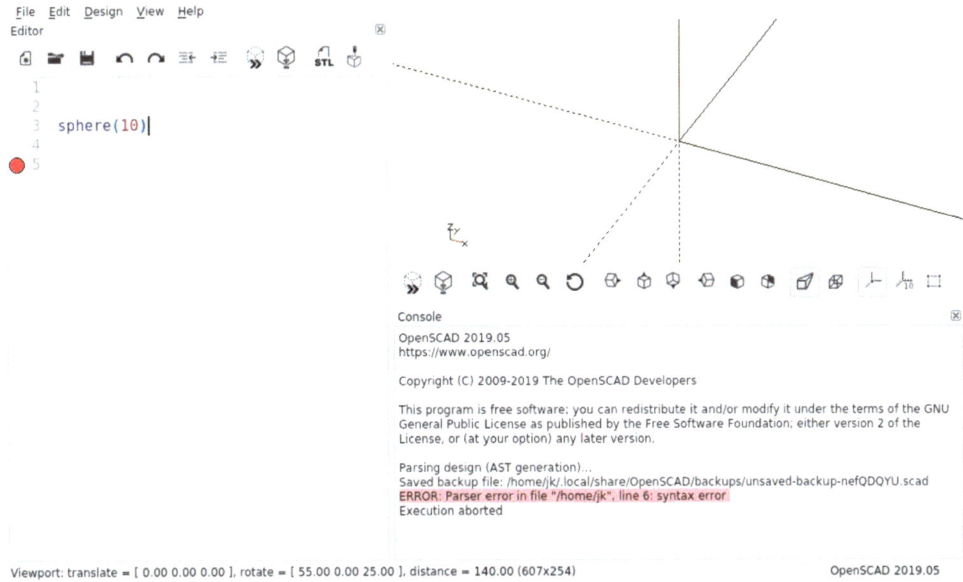

Figure 3.2: Error during preview rendering

Try it out (*F5*). The sphere should now appear with only half of its previous size in the output window. What will happen if we specify both a radius and a diameter?

```
sphere(r = 10, d = 10);
```

If you now run a preview (*F5*), then the sphere does not change and a warning highlighted in yellow is displayed in the console: *Ignoring radius variable 'r' as diameter 'd' is defined too*. So for the sphere, the diameter has priority over the radius if both are given. The order of the parameters does not matter here.

If you have some programming experience, the expression `sphere(r=10);` may remind you of a method call. Unfortunately, in the context of OpenSCAD this intuition is more hindering than useful. It is better to interpret the expression **not** as a method call, but rather as a statement about the existence of a concrete geometry. In this sense, the expression `sphere(r=10);` says something like: *there exists a sphere with radius 10mm*.

So far we have specified the radius of our sphere with a concrete value. If we are sure that we will never need or want to adjust this value again, this is perfectly fine. However, if we want to make the radius of the sphere *configurable* in our model, then we should give the radius its own name. We can do this by using a *variable*:

```
radius_with_a_name = 10;

sphere( r = radius_with_a_name );
```

In larger projects it is useful to collect all configuration variables at the beginning of the model file. This way, you have an overview of all possible settings. In addition, you should get into the habit of commenting the variables (and the geometry where it feels suitable) right away. Single-line comments can be introduced with //. In this case, everything up to the end of the line is considered a comment. If you need more space, you can start a comment block with /* and end it with */:

```
/*
    This is an OpenSCAD test project
    --------------------------------
*/

radius_with_a_name = 10;   // a very important radius

// the main sphere of our model
sphere( r = radius_with_a_name );
```

At this point programming experience can be a hindrance again. Our model looks even more like a typical sequential program now! But this is not the case. A variable in OpenSCAD represents **not** a memory location that could take on different values in the course of a program. Instead, it is again just an existence statement: *there exists the value 10 called "radius_with_a_name"*. What happens if we assign a value to a variable twice? Let's try it out!

```
radius_with_a_name = 10;

sphere( r = radius_with_a_name );

radius_with_a_name = 20;
```

If we now run the preview (*F5*), we see that the sphere is rendered with a radius of 20. At the same time we see a warning in the console output: *sphere radius was assigned on line 1 but was overwritten on line 5.* As you can see, you can only give one value to a variable. OpenSCAD always uses the last value that was assigned (here 20). This also means that a variable does not have to be defined "before" it is used. The "before" is in quotes because there is no temporal "before" in this sense in an OpenSCAD geometry description.

When describing values by variables, one is not limited to using only single values. Let's assume that the dimensions in our model still need a correction value. We could implement this like so:

```
adjustment = 0.7;

main_radius = 10 + adjustment;
margin      =  5 + adjustment;
depth       = 25 + adjustment;


// ... even more configuration variables with adjustment
```

So far so good. Let's assume that we suddenly realize that we also need a correction factor! We could implement that as follows:

```
adjustment        = 0.7;
adjustment_factor = 1.05;

main_radius = (10 + adjustment) * adjustment_factor;
margin      = ( 5 + adjustment) * adjustment_factor;
depth       = (25 + adjustment) * adjustment_factor;
```

You can already see that it's kind of cumbersome to have to update every configuration variable. A more elegant solution is to use a function for the adjustment:

```
adjustment        = 0.7;
adjustment_factor = 1.05;

function adjust(x) = (x + adjustment) * adjustment_factor;

main_radius = adjust(10);
margin      = adjust( 5);
depth       = adjust(25);
```

If we now need to change the adjustment in our example again, then we only need to update the function `adjust(x)`. Function definitions are introduced with the keyword `function`, followed by a unique name for the function (here `adjust`) and a parameter list in round brackets (here `(x)`). The function itself is written after an equal sign and always ends with a semicolon. Apart from our own custom functions, OpenSCAD offers a whole set of predefined functions (e.g. sin(), cos(), round()), most of which we will get to know within the course of this book.

Before we move on to the next section, let's briefly recap what we have learned:

- Geometric primitives have a unique name which is always followed by a list of parameters in round brackets and a terminating semicolon.

- Variables allow values to be given a name and are primarily used to parameterize the model.

- Functions allow mathematical expressions to be given a name such that they can be used in a consistent way throughout the model description.

3.2 Transformations

In the previous section we used the basic shape *sphere* in our model description. Now, for a change, we will use a *cube*:

```
cube(size = 10, center = true);
```

The parameter *size* sets the length of the cube's edges. The parameter *center* defines where the cube has its origin (Figure 3.3).

Like the sphere, the cube is displayed at the origin of the coordinate system. In the output window, the coordinate system is represented by three perpendicular lines, each representing the X-, Y- and Z-axes, respectively. The positive regions of each axis are represented by solid lines. The negative regions are represented by dashed lines. With the shortkey 'CTRL + 2' the coordinate axes can be shown or hidden. Also, pay attention

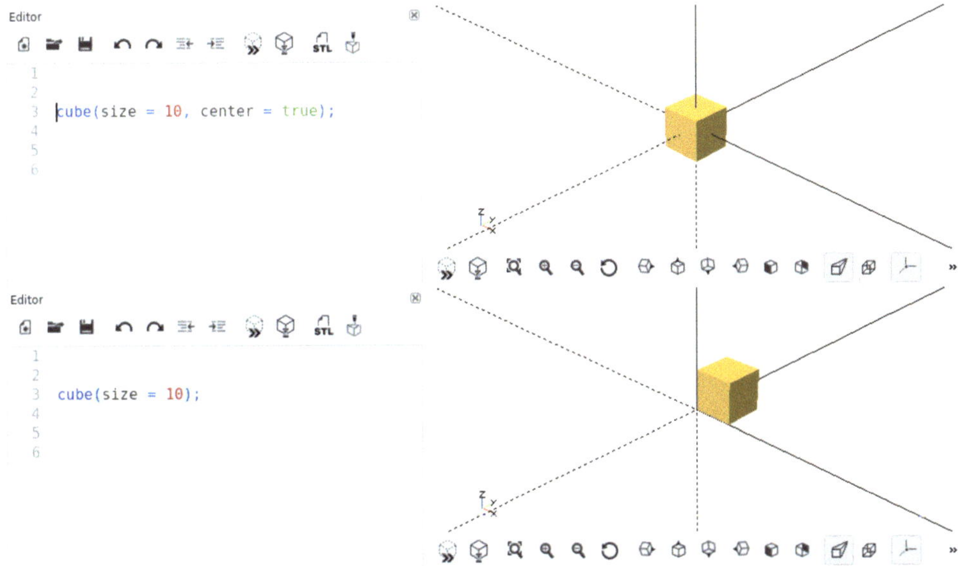

Figure 3.3: A cube with and without the *center* parameter

to the small, labeled coordinate cross at the bottom left of the output window. It serves as an orientation aid.

If we now want to move our cube to another position, we have to use a so-called *transformation*. In this case a translation:

```
translate( [20,0,0] ) cube(10,true);
```

A transformation (here `translate( [20,0,0] )`) always affects the following element. In this case our cube. The transformation *translate* gets a three-dimensional vector as parameter, which describes the desired displacement in X-, Y- and Z-direction. Vectors are written with square brackets in OpenSCAD and the numbers inside a vector are separated by commas.

It is important to emphasize a key concept of the OpenSCAD language here: The entire expression `translate(...) cube(...);` is an **independent** geometric object that can be used like any other basic shape (sphere, cube, etc.)! This means, in particular, that we can prepend further transformations to this new object, e.g. a rotation:

```
rotate( [0,0,45] ) translate( [20,0,0] ) cube(10,true);
```

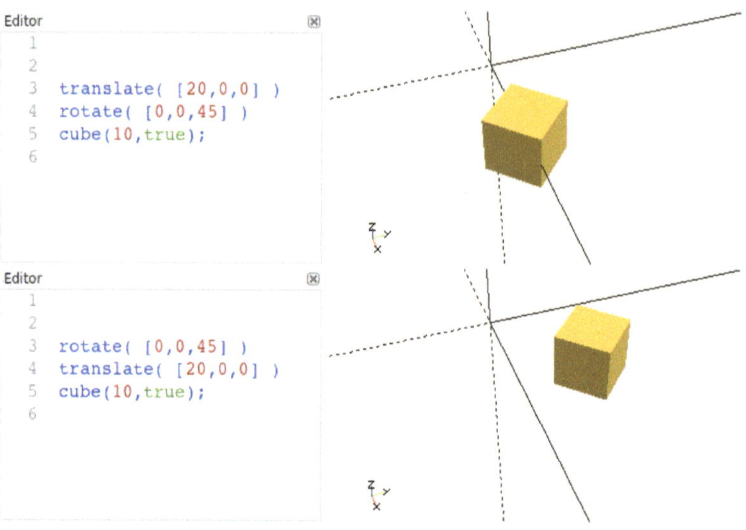

Figure 3.4: The order of transformations matters!

The transformation *rotate* rotates a geometric object around the origin. As parameter the transformation requires a three-dimensional vector. In this case the vector contains the desired rotation angles around the X, Y and Z axis. And again, the entire expression `rotate(...) translate(...) cube(...);` is a new, **independent** geometric object. Since the semicolon marks the end of that object, you can also write the transformations in the lines above the basic shape (here: *cube*) to avoid an overly long line length.

Figure 3.4 illustrates how our final result depends on the order of the transformations. Since the transformations in OpenSCAD always refer to the origin, it makes a big difference whether you move an object first and then rotate it, or vice versa.

Basic geometric shapes and transformations give us roughly the modeling capabilities that we had as children with our toy building blocks. In the next section, we will expand these capabilities significantly.

3.3   Combining Geometries

Let's assume that we want to model a 5mm thick plate with a dimension of 10cm x 5cm. We could do this as follows:

```
1
2  // dimensions in millimeter [width, depth, height]
3  plate = [100,50,5];
4
5  cube( plate );
6
7
8
9
10
11
12
13
14
15
```

Figure 3.5: Basic form *cube* parameterized by a vector

```
// dimensions in millimeter [width, depth, height]
plate = [100,50,5];

cube( plate );
```

We define a three-dimensional vector *plate* containing the dimensions of our plate and pass this vector as a parameter to the basic shape *cube* (Figure 3.5).

Suppose we now want to model four holes at the corners of the plate. Let's start by defining two variables. One for the diameter of the holes and one for the distance of the holes from the edge of the plate:

```
// dimensions in millimeter [width, depth, height]
plate = [100,50,5];

hole_dm     = 6;
hole_margin = 4;

cube( plate );
```

Next, we need to describe what shape our holes should have. The basic shape *cylinder* is suitable for this:

```
// dimensions in mm [width, depth, height]
plate = [100,50,5];

hole_dm     = 6;
hole_margin = 4;
```

```
cube( plate );

cylinder( d = hole_dm, h = plate.z );
```

The parameter *d* of the basic shape *cylinder* sets the diameter, the parameter *h* sets the height. We pass our variable **hole_dm** as *d* and the Z-coordinate of the plate vector as *h*, as **plate.z** contains the thickness of our plate. Instead of **plate.z** we could have written **plate[2]** as well.

The cylinder has now the right dimensions but is still in the wrong place (Figure 3.6). Moreover, it is hard to distinguish from the plate. Let's move the cylinder and give it a different color:

```
// dimensions in mm [width, depth, height]
plate = [100,50,5];

hole_dm     = 6;
hole_margin = 4;

cube( plate );

translate
([
  hole_margin + hole_dm / 2,
  hole_margin + hole_dm / 2,
  0
])
color( "red" )
cylinder( d = hole_dm, h = plate.z );
```

```
 1
 2   // dimensions in mm [width, depth, height]
 3   plate = [100,50,5];
 4
 5   hole_margin = 4;
 6   hole_dm     = 6;
 7
 8   cube( plate );
 9
10   cylinder( d = hole_dm, h = plate.z );
11
12
13
14
15
```

Figure 3.6: Basic form *cylinder* at the origin of the coordinate system

First, we apply the transformation *color* and use it to color the cylinder red. We then move the red cylinder to the lower left corner of the plate using the transformation *translate*. To keep our model description a bit clearer, we have arranged the parameter of the translate transformation vertically.

3.3.1 Boolean Operators

Before we take care of the cylinders needed in the other three corners, we create our first hole in the plate. This is done with a so-called *Boolean operation*, which can combine two or more geometries. In OpenSCAD there are three types of Boolean operation available: *difference, union,* and *intersection.* For our hole we need the difference operation because we want to "subtract" the cylinder from the plate:

```
// dimensions in mm [width, depth, height]
plate = [100,50,5];

hole_margin = 4;
hole_dm     = 6;

difference() {

  cube( plate );

  translate( [hole_margin + hole_dm / 2, hole_margin + hole_dm / 2, 0] )
  color( "red" )
  cylinder( d = hole_dm, h = plate.z );

}
```

Just like a transformation, a Boolean operation (here: *difference()*) affects the following element. Since Boolean operations combine multiple geometries, it would make little sense if the subsequent element consisted of only a single geometry - even though this would be valid in principle. To have more than one subsequent element a *geometry set* is used. It is defined by enclosing one or more geometric objects with a pair of curly braces { ... }. In case of the difference operation all geometries following the first geometry in the set are subtracted from that first geometry.

Figure 3.7 shows that our first hole is, unfortunately, not without errors. The surface at the location of the hole shows strange defects. Especially when you change the view in

```
 1  // dimensions in mm [width, depth, height]
 2  plate = [100,50,5];
 3
 4  hole_margin = 4;
 5  hole_dm     = 6;
 6
 7  difference() {
 8
 9      cube( plate );
10
11      translate
12      ([
13          hole_margin + hole_dm / 2,
14          hole_margin + hole_dm / 2,
15          0
16      ])
17      color( "red" )
18      cylinder( d = hole_dm, h = plate.z );
19
20  }
21
```

Figure 3.7: Defective surface after difference operation

the output window with the mouse. These defects are caused by rounding errors during the difference calculation, as the top and bottom sides of our cylinder are flush with the top and bottom side of the plate. To fix the problem, we need to increase the height of the cylinder a tiny bit while at the same time move it down a bit so that the cylinder protrudes both top and bottom of the plate:

```
// dimensions in mm [width, depth, height]
plate = [100,50,5];

hole_dm     = 6;
hole_margin = 4;

difference() {

  cube( plate );

  translate( [hole_margin + hole_dm / 2, hole_margin + hole_dm / 2, -1] )
  color( "red" )
  cylinder( d = hole_dm, h = plate.z + 2);

}
```

Now the resulting hole looks clean (Figure 3.8). To check the position of the cylinder you can temporarily prefix the cylinder object with a # in the model description and re-run the preview. This will display the cylinder with a semi-transparent red color.

Now we can finally take care of the other three holes. To do this, we simply copy our existing cylinder three times and adjust the position in each case:

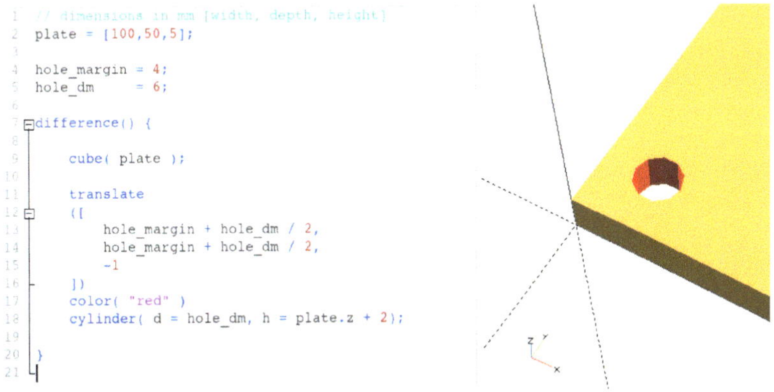

Figure 3.8: Clean difference operation

```
// dimensions in mm [width, depth, height]
plate = [100,50,5];

hole_dm     = 6;
hole_margin = 4;

difference() {

  cube( plate );

  abs_margin = hole_margin + hole_dm / 2;

  // lower left hole
  translate
  ([
    abs_margin,
    abs_margin,
    -1
  ])
  color( "red" )
  cylinder( d = hole_dm, h = plate.z + 2);

  // lower right hole
  translate
  ([
    plate.x - abs_margin,
    abs_margin,
    -1
  ])
```

```
  color( "red" )
  cylinder( d = hole_dm, h = plate.z + 2);

  // upper left hole
  translate
  ([
    abs_margin,
    plate.y - abs_margin,
    -1
  ])
  color( "red" )
  cylinder( d = hole_dm, h = plate.z + 2);

  // upper right hole
  translate
  ([
    plate.x - abs_margin,
    plate.y - abs_margin,
    -1
  ])
  color( "red" )
  cylinder( d = hole_dm, h = plate.z + 2);
}
```

The geometry set of the difference operation now contains five objects. Our plate
followed by four cylinders. This leads to the desired result (Figure 3.9). However, our
geometry description is now very extensive and somewhat convoluted.

Figure 3.9: A plate with four holes and a lot of copied definitions

3.3.2 Loops

Whenever you find yourself copying a definition block multiple times, only to change it minimally each time, you have a strong indication that there is probably a better way to describe the current geometry. This is also true here. Instead of copying the cylinders four times, we can describe the four instances using a loop:

```
// dimensions in mm [width, depth, height]
plate = [100,50,5];

hole_dm     = 6;
hole_margin = 4;

difference() {

  cube( plate );

  abs_margin = hole_margin + hole_dm / 2;
  x_values   = [abs_margin, plate.x - abs_margin];
  y_values   = [abs_margin, plate.y - abs_margin];

  // holes
  for (x = x_values, y = y_values)
    translate( [x, y, -1] )
    color( "red" )
    cylinder( d = hole_dm, h = plate.z + 2);

}
```

Loops in OpenSCAD begin with the keyword *for* followed by the definition of one or more loop variables in round brackets. The loop variables can be assigned either an *array* or a *range*. We have already learned about arrays in the form of vectors. They do not differ in their definition. A range looks very similar to an array: `[start_value :` `end_value]` or `[start_value : increment : end_value]`. You can think of a range as an implicit array where you only specify start and end values while the values in between are calculated automatically. If no increment is specified, an increment of 1 is assumed.

Just like transformations and Boolean operations, for-loops operate on the subsequent element, which is used as a template to create a new geometric object for each possible combination of the loop variables. At those places where the loop variables are used in the template, the corresponding values from the associated array or range are substituted. The "result" of a for-loop is **not** a geometry set, but a single, unified geometry.

Our example uses the *x_values* and *y_values* arrays, which are assigned to the loop variables *x* and *y*. Here is a version that uses two ranges:

```
// dimensions in mm [width, depth, height]
plate = [100,50,5];

hole_dm     = 6;
hole_margin = 4;

difference() {

  cube( plate );

  abs_margin  = hole_margin + hole_dm / 2;
  x_hole_dist = plate.x - 2 * abs_margin;
  y_hole_dist = plate.y - 2 * abs_margin;
  x_values    = [abs_margin : x_hole_dist : plate.x - abs_margin];
  y_values    = [abs_margin : y_hole_dist : plate.y - abs_margin];

  // holes
  for (x = x_values, y = y_values)
    translate( [x, y, -1] )
    color( "red" )
    cylinder( d = hole_dm, h = plate.z + 2);

}
```

Using two ranges is a bit more involved than using two arrays as we have to calculate the appropriate increments *x_hole_dist* and *y_hole_dist* first. In the next section we will benefit from this extra effort. Before we continue it is worth having a look at the *Customizer* (Figure 3.10).

Our variables *plate, hole_dm* and *hole_margin* were automatically recognized and inserted as controls in the Customizer. If the Customizer does not show anything, it helps to let the preview run again. Click on the small triangle in front of *Parameters* if necessary. You can now save and load different configurations as *Presets*. However, this functionality only works if you have already saved the geometry description as a .scad file. The presets themselves are saved in a second file, which has the same name as the .scad file, but ends in .json.

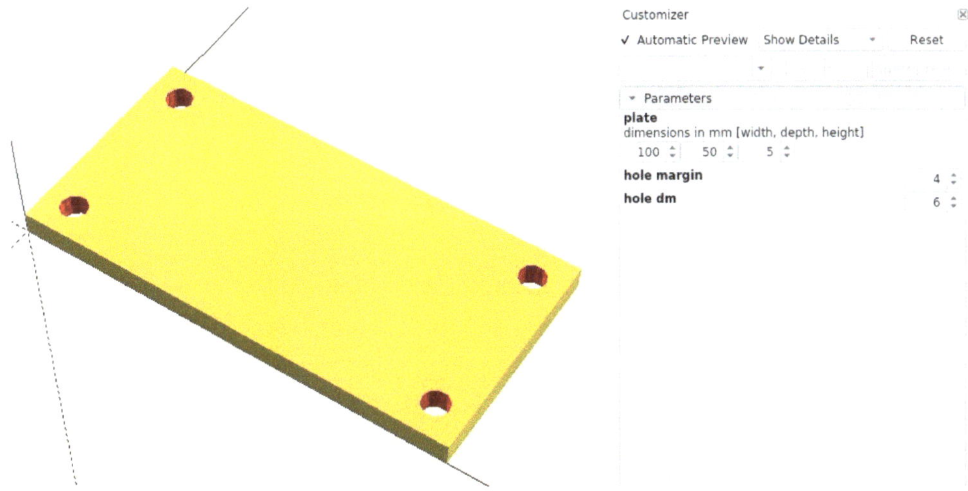

Figure 3.10: Easy customization of our geometry with the Customizer

3.3.3 Modules

The geometry description of our plate is now pretty much finished. What we are still missing is the ability to use our plate multiple times without having to copy our geometry description. For this purpose we can package a geometry description inside a *module*:

```
module hole_plate( size, hole_dm, hole_margin) {

  difference() {

    cube( size );

    abs_margin  = hole_margin + hole_dm / 2;
    x_hole_dist = size.x - 2*abs_margin;
    y_hole_dist = size.y - 2*abs_margin;
    x_values    = [abs_margin : x_hole_dist : size.x - abs_margin];
    y_values    = [abs_margin : y_hole_dist : size.y - abs_margin];

    // holes
    for (x = x_values, y = y_values)
    translate( [x, y, -1] )
    color( "red" )
    cylinder( d = hole_dm, h = size.z + 2);
  }
}
```

```
hole_plate( [100,50,5], 6, 4 );

translate( [0,60,0] )
hole_plate( size = [50,50,5], hole_dm = 3, hole_margin = 2 );

translate( [60,60,0] )
hole_plate( [50,50,5], hole_dm = 5, hole_margin = 5 );
```

In OpenSCAD a module definition starts with the keyword *module*. It is followed by the name of the module (here: *hole_plate*) and its parameter list in round brackets. We do not have to specify what type the parameters have. The type of the parameters is automatically determined by OpenSCAD based on their usage. Thus, in our example, the parameter *size* is a three-dimensional vector, while *hole_dm* and *hole_margin* are simple numbers. The content of a module is a geometry set enclosed by curly brackets - just as we have already seen with Boolean operators.

Once you have defined the module, you can use it like one of the basic shapes (sphere, cube, etc.). In our example, we have created three plates, two of which we have arranged using translate transformations (Figure 3.11).

Within the module, we have taken our original geometry description and merely made the formerly global variables the module's parameters. We used the last version of our description from the previous section. It allows us to easily extend the functionality of our module such that we can parameterize the number of holes:

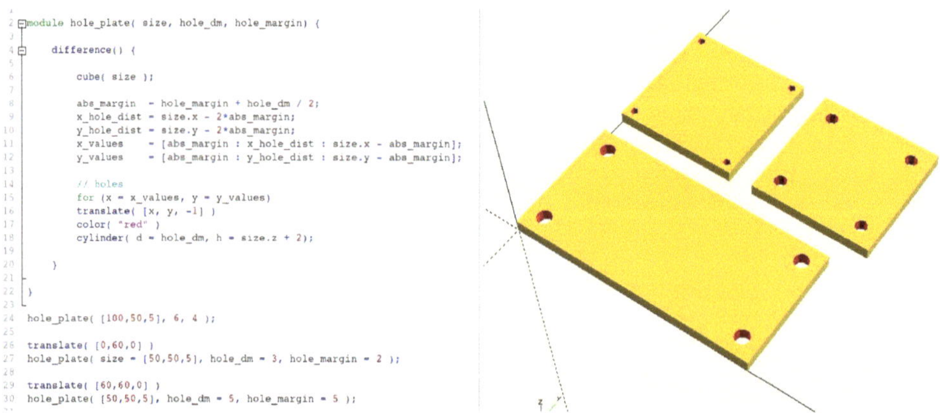

Figure 3.11: Easy reusability through modules

```
module hole_plate( size, hole_dm, hole_margin, hole_count = [2,2] ) {

  difference() {

    cube( size );

    abs_margin  = hole_margin + hole_dm/2;
    x_hole_dist = (size.x - 2*abs_margin) / (hole_count.x - 1);
    y_hole_dist = (size.y - 2*abs_margin) / (hole_count.y - 1);
    x_values    = [abs_margin : x_hole_dist : size.x - abs_margin + 0.1];
    y_values    = [abs_margin : y_hole_dist : size.y - abs_margin + 0.1];

    // holes
    for (x = x_values, y = y_values)
      translate( [x, y, -1] )
      color( "red" )
      cylinder( d = hole_dm, h = size.z + 2);

  }

}

hole_plate( [100,50,5], 6, 4 );

translate( [0,60,0] )
hole_plate(
  size        = [50,50,5],
  hole_dm     = 3,
  hole_margin = 2,
  hole_count  = [4,6]
);

translate( [60,60,0] )
hole_plate( [50,50,5], hole_dm = 5, hole_margin = 5, hole_count = [4,3] );
```

We have added a parameter *hole_count* to our module and given it a default value
(here: [2,2], a two-dimensional vector). Since we used two ranges (*x_values* and
y_values) for the loop variables, we only need to adjust the increments *x_hole_dist*
and *y_hole_dist* to create the desired number of holes in X- and Y-direction. Again,
rounding errors can get in our way. Therefore we also have to adjust the end value of
the ranges slightly (+ 0.1). As the actual values used in the for-loop are determined
solely on the basis of the increments, we do not cause any inaccuracy in our design with
this adjustment.

```
module hole_plate( size, hole_dm, hole_margin, hole_count = [2,2] ) {

    difference() {

        cube( size );

        abs_margin  = hole_margin + hole_dm/2;
        x_hole_dist = (size.x - 2*abs_margin) / (hole_count.x - 1);
        y_hole_dist = (size.y - 2*abs_margin) / (hole_count.y - 1);
        x_values    = [abs_margin : x_hole_dist : size.x - abs_margin + 0.1];
        y_values    = [abs_margin : y_hole_dist : size.y - abs_margin + 0.1];

        // holes
        for (x = x_values, y = y_values)
        translate( [x, y, -1] )
        color( "red" )
        cylinder( d = hole_dm, h = size.z + 2);

    }

}

hole_plate( [100,50,5], 6, 4 );

translate( [0,60,0] )
hole_plate(
    size        = [50,50,5],
    hole_dm     = 3,
    hole_margin = 2,
    hole_count  = [4,6]
);

translate( [60,60,0] )
hole_plate( [50,50,5], hole_dm = 5, hole_margin = 5, hole_count = [4,3] );
```

Figure 3.12: Simple extension of our module

Since we have defined the new *hole_count* parameter of our module with a default value, the module is "backwards compatible". Thus, the first use of our module, in which we do not specify a value for *hole_count*, has not changed (Figure 3.12).

3.3.4 Conditional Description

Our module still has a few blemishes. If the parameter *hole_count* contains the value 1, then the calculation of the corresponding hole distance contains a division by 0. This is not good and we should definitely take care of it. Maybe we should just make a single, centered hole if count is 1? To achieve this, we need to make both the calculation of the hole distances (*x_hole_dist* and *y_hole_dist*) and the definition of the value ranges (*x_values* and *y_values*) conditional on the *hole_count* parameter:

```
module hole_plate( size, hole_dm, hole_margin, hole_count = [2,2] ) {

  difference() {

    cube( size );

    abs_margin  = hole_margin + hole_dm / 2;

    x_hole_dist = hole_count.x > 1 ?
                  (size.x - 2 * abs_margin) / (hole_count.x - 1) : 0;
```

```
    y_hole_dist = hole_count.y > 1 ?
                 (size.y - 2 * abs_margin) / (hole_count.y - 1) : 0;

    x_values    = hole_count.x > 1 ?
            [abs_margin : x_hole_dist : size.x - abs_margin + 0.1] :
              [size.x / 2];

    y_values    = hole_count.y > 1 ?
                 [abs_margin : y_hole_dist : size.y - abs_margin + 0.1] :
                 [size.y / 2];

    // holes
    for (x = x_values, y = y_values)
    translate( [x, y, -1] )
    color( "red" )
    cylinder( d = hole_dm, h = size.z + 2);

  }

}

hole_plate( [100,50,5], 6, 4 );

translate( [0,60,0] )
hole_plate(
  size        = [50,50,5],
  hole_dm     = 3,
  hole_margin = 2,
  hole_count  = [1,1]
);

translate( [60,60,0] )
hole_plate( [50,50,5], hole_dm = 5, hole_margin = 5, hole_count = [2,1] );
```

The conditional parts of the geometry description use the *question mark operator*. In general, this operator has the structure **a ? b : c**. The part *a* is always a yes or no question (here: "is hole_count.x greater than 1"). If the answer is *yes*, part *b* is taken as value, if the answer is *no*, part *c* is taken instead.

If you have some programming experience, you may have first thought about using an *if* statement to make the above case distinction. Again, "normal" programming intuition is a hindrance here. After all, we can only assign a value once to a variable in OpenSCAD! The following expression would therefore **not** work as expected in OpenSCAD:

```
x_hole_dist = 0;
if (hole_count.x > 1) {
  x_hole_dist = (size.x - 2 * abs_margin) / (hole_count.x - 1);
}
```

Nevertheless, there are also *if*-statements in OpenSCAD. You can use it to include or exclude whole parts of the geometry description. We can use it in our example to remove yet another flaw in our module. At the moment, a number of 0 or any negative value would also result in a single hole. This doesn't seem to make sense. If we specify a 0 for the number of holes, then we obviously don't want a hole at all:

```
module hole_plate( size, hole_dm, hole_margin, hole_count = [2,2] ) {

  if (hole_count.x == 0 || hole_count.y == 0) {

    cube( size );

  } else {

    difference() {

      cube( size );

      abs_margin  = hole_margin + hole_dm / 2;

      x_hole_dist = hole_count.x > 1 ?
                  (size.x - 2 * abs_margin) / (hole_count.x - 1) : 0;

      y_hole_dist = hole_count.y > 1 ?
                  (size.y - 2 * abs_margin) / (hole_count.y - 1) : 0;

      x_values = hole_count.x > 1 ?
              [abs_margin : x_hole_dist : size.x - abs_margin + 0.1] :
              [size.x / 2];

      y_values = hole_count.y > 1 ?
              [abs_margin : y_hole_dist : size.y - abs_margin + 0.1] :
              [size.y / 2];

      // holes
      for (x = x_values, y = y_values)
      translate( [x, y, -1] )
      color( "red" )
      cylinder( d = hole_dm, h = size.z + 2);
```

```
      }
    }
  }
}

hole_plate( [100,50,5], 6, 4 );

translate( [0,60,0] )
hole_plate(
    size     = [50,50,5],
    hole_dm    = 3,
    hole_margin = 2,
    hole_count   = [0,1]
);

translate( [60,60,0] )
hole_plate( [50,50,5], hole_dm = 5, hole_margin = 5, hole_count = [2,1] );
```

So here we distinguish right at the beginning whether we want to model a plate with or without holes and branch our geometry description accordingly. Equality is expressed with the double equal sign (==). The two vertical lines (||) have the meaning of a logical "or" in the sense of "only one of the two questions must be answered with yes".

3.4   External Geometry

Let's say we want to reuse our plate in another project. It would be a bad idea to simply copy the geometry description into the new project file. Instead, OpenSCAD offers two commands to include other .scad files into a project:

```
include <hole_plate.scad>;
```

The *include* command imports another .scad file (here: *hole_plate.scad*) completely into the current geometry description. This means that also the three test plates we defined below our module would appear in the new geometry description. To avoid this, OpenSCAD also has the *use* command as an alternative:

```
use <hole_plate.scad>;
```

If you import geometry with *use* instead of *include*, only the modules and functions from the other `.scad` file are imported, but no global variables or instantiations of geometries. The file specified within the angle brackets must either be located in the same directory as the file of the current geometry description, or in the *Library Folder* of OpenSCAD. You can use the menu entry *File -> Show Library Folder* to display the library folder and store your geometry libraries there. On the Internet you can find a number of very excellent geometry libraries for OpenSCAD. The library directory is the place where you have to copy them in order to use them.

If you want to use an external geometry in OpenSCAD that has a different format than `.scad`, you can use the *import* keyword.

```
import("logo.svg");
```

The imported geometry can then be used like a basic shape (sphere, cube, etc.) or a module (e.g. `translate(...) import("logo.svg");`). OpenSCAD supports DXF and SVG as two-dimensional formats and STL, OFF, AMF and 3MF as three-dimensional formats.

3.5 Summary

Congratulations! You now know all essential concepts and functionalities of OpenSCAD. Everything else is really "just" details. In the following projects, we will practice and deepen our understanding of these concepts and gradually work our way through the remaining functionality. You will see that your understanding of the material will gradually improve with each project, so that you will soon have a clear understanding of how to get from an idea to a finished geometry description.

Project 1: Shelf Bracket

In this project we construct a shelf bracket. Both the lengths of the two sides and the size and number of the holes will be freely adjustable.

4.1   What's new?

We will learn about *union* as a new Boolean operation. In addition, we will use a few mathematical functions (root, power and arc cosine) from OpenSCAD and learn more about modules. Last but not least, we will look at the projection function as we use it to create drilling templates for our shelf bracket.

4.2   Let's go

To start, let's create an empty module *shelf_bracket* and think about what parameters we need. We want to be able to change the length of each side, as well as the size and

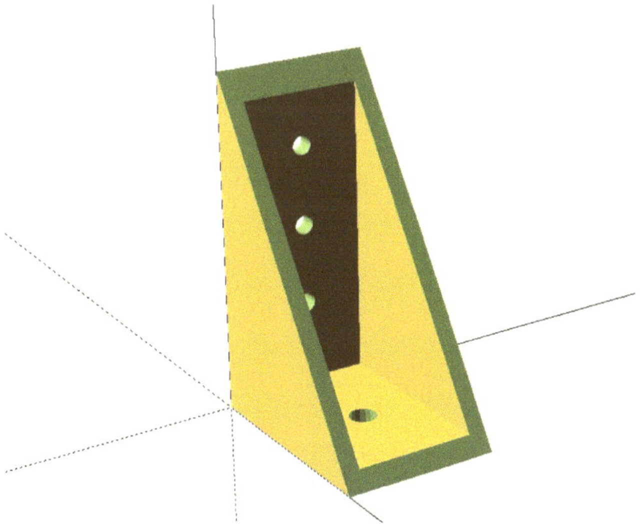

Figure 4.1: shelf bracket

number of holes. In addition, our bracket will have a width and we need to know what material thickness the bracket should have. That's a lot of parameters! To keep our parameter list short, we can combine the values of each side (length, hole diameter, number of holes) into a three-dimensional vector:

```
/*
    module shelf_bracket

    parameters:
    - side_a    is a vector [length, hole diameter, number of holes]
    - side_b    is a vector [length, hole diameter, number of holes]
    - width     refers to the width of the bracket
    - thickness refers to the material thickness of the bracket
 */

module shelf_bracket( side_a, side_b, width, thickness ) {

}

shelf_bracket(
  side_a    = [50, 6, 1],
  side_b    = [75, 4, 3],
  width     = 35,
  thickness = 4
);
```

Above our module we have written a multiline comment (/* ... */) that briefly explains what parameters there are and what kind of input these parameters expect. Even if nobody else will use your module, such a comment is useful. If you need a shelf bracket again in 6 months, you will be glad about the helpful comment! Below the module *shelf_bracket* we have instantiated the module once with concrete values. Without this instance, we would not see any geometry in the output window as we develop our module step by step. In addition, we can use the instance to change the parameters every now and then during development to check whether our geometry description behaves as expected.

If you look at the shelf bracket in figure 4.1, you will notice that the two sides of the bracket are basically the same. They consist of a plate and evenly distributed holes along the central axis. We need this geometry for both sides. Therefore, it is worth encapsulating one side within a module and use it twice. Since we need this module only for the bracket, we define it **inside** the module *shelf_bracket* as submodule *xhole_plate* and then use the submodule for side A and side B of the bracket:

```
module shelf_bracket( side_a, side_b, width, thickness, ) {

    module xhole_plate(size, h_dm, h_num, margin) {

        difference(){

            cube(size);

            h_distance = (size.x - margin) / (h_num + 1);

            for (x = [1:h_num])
            translate ([
                margin + x * h_distance,
                size.y/2,
                -1
            ]) cylinder( d = h_dm, h = size.z + 2, $fn=18);
        }
    }

    // side A
    xhole_plate(
        [side_a[0], width, thickness],
        side_a[1],
        side_a[2],
        thickness
    );

    // side B
    translate([thickness,0,0])
    rotate([0,-90,0])
    xhole_plate(
        [side_b[0], width, thickness],
        side_b[1],
        side_b[2],
        thickness
    );
}
```

The submodule *xhole_plate* gets as parameters the size of the side part as a three-dimensional vector (*size*), the diameter (*h_dm*) and the number (*h_num*) of the holes as well as a *margin*. The latter is needed as the surface area of the sides is reduced by the thickness of the material at the point where the two sides of the bracket meet.

Since we want to distribute our holes along this surface, we have to take this reduction into account. Theoretically, we could have derived the material thickness from the parameter *size* (*size.z*). The use of an extra parameter simply makes it easier to read and understand.

We model the plate with a simple cube, passing it the *size* parameter (`cube(size);`). We create the holes with a for-loop and then subtract them from the plate using the Boolean difference operation. In this example we let the for-loop run from 1 to the number of holes (`x = [1:h_num]`) and calculate the actual position of the respective hole directly in the translate transformation inside the loop (`margin + x * h_distance`). We always start with the margin and then add the appropriate number of hole distances. We have defined the hole distance (`h_distance`) before the loop. For this we divided the available length (length of the side minus margin) by the number of hole interspaces (number of holes plus 1). For the holes themselves, we use a cylinder to which we assign the parameter *h_dm* as the diameter *d*. We determine the height *h* from the height of the plate (*size.z*) and two millimeters allowance, so that our hole will be clean. Matching this allowance, we put a value of -1 (i.e. half the allowance) as z-shift in the translate transformation. As a result, the cylinder protrudes exactly 1 millimeter above and below the plate. The third parameter *$fn=18* of the cylinder is new. It is a "special variable" of OpenSCAD with which you can set the level of detail of curved geometries. The larger the value of *$fn* is, the finer the geometry becomes. Though, keep in mind that values of more than 100 for the variable *$fn* are practically never needed and would only make the geometry unnecessarily complex. You can also set the variable *$fn* "globally". In this case it influences all curved geometries of your model. However, experience shows that it is better to use it specifically where you want to increase the level of detail instead of increasing the level of detail everywhere.

Directly below the module definition of *xhole_plate* we use the module for the two sides A and B. Since side B is perpendicular to side A, we need to rotate it by 90 degrees. In this specific case it is minus 90 degrees, because we want to rotate counterclockwise around the Y-axis. After the rotation, the position of side B is still not quite right. We have to move it by the material thickness along the X axis. Otherwise, side A would become too long.

Our shelf bracket already looks pretty acceptable by now (Figure 4.2) and changing the parameters demonstrates that our geometry description behaves as expected. What we

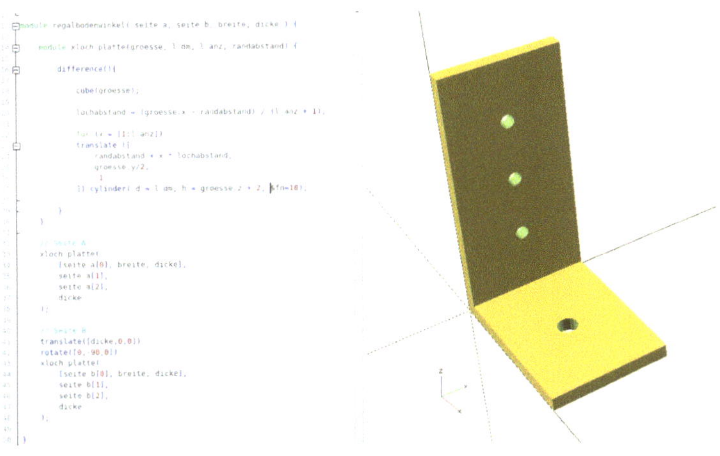

Figure 4.2: Side parts of the bracket created by the submodule

are still missing are two stringers to make our bracket more stable. We first create the stringers from two boxes (*cube*), which we define below sides A and B in our module *shelf_bracket*:

```
module shelf_bracket( side_a, side_b, width, thickness ) {

    module xhole_plate(size, h_dm, h_num, margin) {
        /* ... */
    }

    // side A
    xhole_plate(
        [side_a[0], width, thickness],
        side_a[1],
        side_a[2],
        thickness
    );

    // side B
    translate([thickness,0,0])
    rotate([0,-90,0])
    xhole_plate(
        [side_b[0], width, thickness],
        side_b[1],
        side_b[2],
        thickness
    );
```

```
    // stringer
    cube( [side_a[0], thickness, side_b[0]] );

    translate( [0, width - thickness, 0] )
    cube( [side_a[0], thickness, side_b[0]] );
}
```

From a purely technical point of view, our stringers already serve their purpose (Figure 4.3). However, it would be nicer if our shelf bracket had tapered stringers. We can achieve this by subtracting a suitably rotated box from our existing bracket. To make this possible, we need to combine our previous geometry description, which consists of four individual geometries (two times *xhole_plates* and two *cubes*) into a single geometry. This can be done using the Boolean union operation:

```
module shelf_bracket( side_a, side_b, width, thickness ) {

    module xhole_plate(size, h_dm, h_num, margin) {
        /* ... */
    }

    union() {

        // side A
        xhole_plate(
            /* ... */
        );

        // side B
        translate([thickness,0,0])
        rotate([0,-90,0])
        xhole_plate(
            /* ... */
        );

        // stringer
        cube( [side_a[0], thickness, side_b[0]] );

        translate( [0, width - thickness, 0] )
        cube( [side_a[0], thickness, side_b[0]] );
    }
}
```

Like with the Boolean difference operation, we combine the individual geometries by surrounding them with a set of curly brackets ({ ... }). Instead of the keyword

```
    }

    // Seite A
    xloch_platte(
        [seite_a[0], breite, dicke],
        seite_a[1],
        seite_a[2],
        dicke
    );

    // Seite B
    translate([dicke,0,0])
    rotate([0,-90,0])
    xloch_platte(
        [seite_b[0], breite, dicke],
        seite_b[1],
        seite_b[2],
        dicke
    );

    // Wangen
    cube( [seite_a[0], dicke, seite_b[0]] );

    translate( [0, breite-dicke, 0] )
    cube( [seite_a[0], dicke, seite_b[0]] );

}

regalbodenwinkel(
    seite_a = [50, 6, 1],
    seite_b = [75, 4, 3],
    breite  = 35,
    dicke   = 4
);
```

Figure 4.3: Raw bracket stringers

difference, we now use the keyword *union*. Having combined our four geometries this way we can now subtract a rotated box to create the desired taper of the stringers.

We now need to know how big this rotated box must be and at what angle it must be tilted (Figure 4.4). Here vague memories of math lessons can help us. According to Pythagoras the sum of the squares of the sides is equal to the square of the main side in a right triangle. So if you take the square root of the sum of the side squares, you get the length of the diagonal you are looking for. The angle can be determined by the arc cosine. As you can look up on, e.g., Wikipedia, the cosine of an angle is equal to the adjacent divided by the hypotenuse. Here, the hypotenuse is our diagonal, and the *adjacent* is the side against which the angle lies (as opposed to the *opposite*, which lies opposite to the angle). We can calculate both values, the length of the diagonal and the

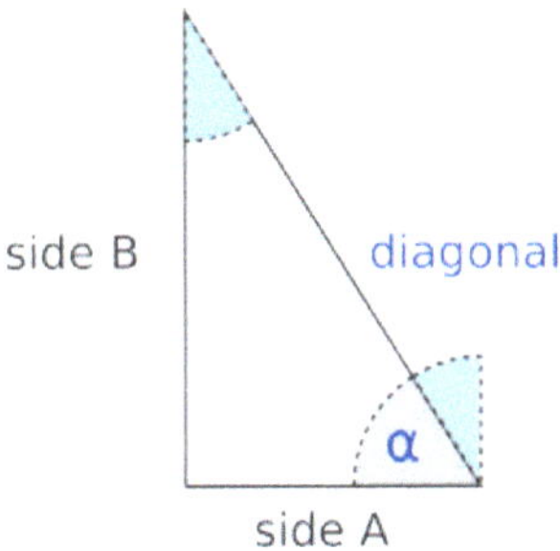

Figure 4.4: We are looking for the diagonal and the angle

angle of the diagonal, with the mathematical functions provided by OpenSCAD and then use them for the correct positioning and rotation of the box:

```
module shelf_bracket( side_a, side_b, width, thickness ) {

    module xhole_plate(size, h_dm, h_num, margin) {
        /* ... */
    }

    difference() {

        union() {

            // side A
            xhole_plate(
                /* ... */
            );

            // side B
            translate([thickness,0,0])
            rotate([0,-90,0])
            xhole_plate(
                /* ... */
            );

            // stringer
            cube( [side_a[0], thickness, side_b[0]] );

            translate( [0, width - thickness, 0] )
            cube( [side_a[0], thickness, side_b[0]] );
        }

        diag  = sqrt( pow(side_a[0], 2) + pow(side_b[0], 2) );
        angle = asin( side_a[0] / diag );

        translate( [side_a[0], -1, 0] )
        rotate( [0, -angle, 0] )
        cube( [diag, width + 2, diag + 2] );
    }
}
```

Below the geometry set of the *union* operation we first calculate our diagonal and our angle. The function *sqrt* calculates the square root and the function *pow* calculates the power of a number. For the power function the first parameter is the number (here: side_a[0] or side_b[0]) you want to exponentiate and the second parameter is the exponent (here: 2). We calculate the angle with the help of the arc cosine (*acos*) as described above from the quotient of the adjacent and the hypotenuse (here: `side_a[0]` divided by `diag`). Subsequently we create a box (*cube*) which is *diag* long, *width + 2* wide and *diag + 2* high. Again, we added some small allowance of two millimeters to both width and height so that our difference operation will perform cleanly later. We rotate the box around the Y axis counterclockwise (hence the -). As angle we do not use the angle we calculated directly, but 90 degrees minus the angle. This is because we actually need the angle that is shaded blue in Figure 4.4. If you remember your math class particularly well, you might now argue that we should have taken the arc sine right then, since it provides the *alternate angle* of the angle we need. And you would be right!

After we have rotated our box, all we have to do is move it to the correct position. This is done with a translate transformation. As expected, we shift our box by the length of side A along the X-axis. The shift of -1 along the Y-axis serves to ensure a clean difference operation and matches the allowance of 2 millimeters in width. We do not need to worry about the addition in height at this point, since it is sufficient if the box overhangs our bracket in the tilting direction.

Now that the box is in the right position, we can finally subtract it from our bracket geometry. To do this, we enclose the union we created earlier and the box we just created in a pair of curly brackets again (`{ ... }`) and prepend the Boolean difference operation to the whole thing. Done!

A hint: if we want to check the position of our box without having to detach it from the Boolean difference operation, we can temporarily prepend a # to the box (*cube*). If we now run a preview, the box will be displayed in a semi-transparent color (Figure 4.5).

4.3   Create drilling templates

Let's assume we have printed our shelf bracket with a 3D printer and now want to mount it onto the wall. Wouldn't it be handy if we now had a drilling template? We can create such a template by using a 3D to 2D projection, which is available in OpenSCAD via the projection transform:

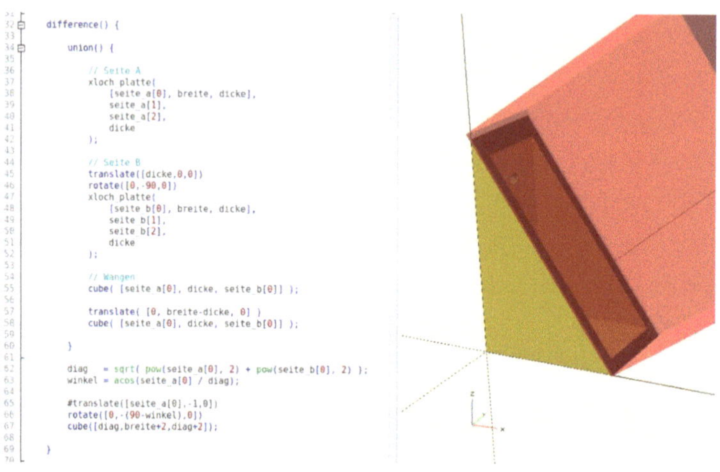

Figure 4.5: Box for tapering the stringers. Made visible by means of #

```
/* ... */

projection(cut = true)
shelf_bracket(
  side_a    = [50, 6, 1],
  side_b    = [75, 4, 3],
  width     = 35,
  thickness = 4
);
```

The projection transform acts like every transformation on the following element and projects it onto the X-Y plane. This results in something like the two-dimensional shadow of the geometry. If you pass the parameter *cut = true* to the projection transform (as we do here), then the geometry is cut in the X-Y plane and only the cut is displayed. In the case of our shelf bracket, both variants lead to the same result. By the way, in order for the section to really be displayed as 2D geometry, you have to trigger a full rendering (*F6*) of the geometry and not just a preview (*F5*). After rendering (*F6*) the 2D geometry can be exported as SVG (*File -> Export -> Export as SVG*) and printed with a graphics program like Inkscape.

If we now also want to have a drilling template of side B, we must rotate our bracket by 90 degrees counterclockwise around the Y axis:

```
/* ... */

projection(cut = true)
rotate( [0, -90, 0] )
shelf_bracket(
    side_a    = [50, 6, 1],
    side_b    = [75, 4, 3],
    width     = 35,
    thickness = 4
);
```

We could leave it at that and comment the lines with the projection and rotation in and out as needed. Alternatively, we can define a special module that can switch between 3D geometry and drilling templates on demand:

```
/* ... */

module output(templates = false) {

    if (templates) {

        projection(cut = true)
        children(0);

        translate( [-0.01, 0, 0] )
        projection(cut = true)
        rotate( [0, -90, 0] )
        children(0);

    } else {

        children(0);

    }

}

output(templates = false)
shelf_bracket(
    side_a    = [50, 6, 1],
    side_b    = [75, 4, 3],
    width     = 35,
    thickness = 4
);
```

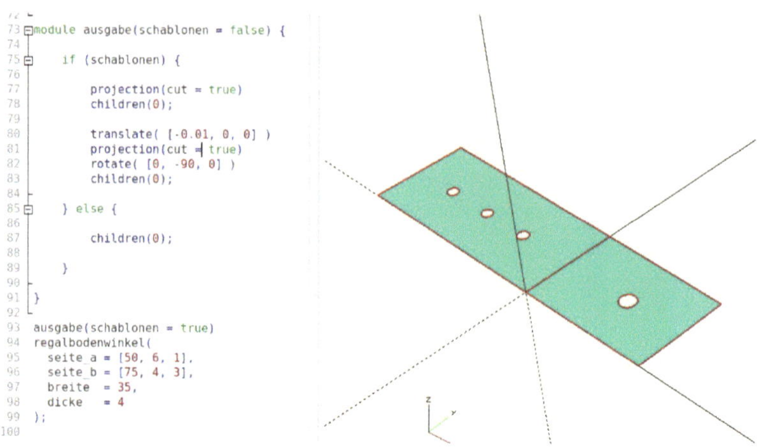

Figure 4.6: Generation of drilling templates by means of *projection*

The module *output* has a parameter *templates*. If it is set to *true*, then the drilling templates of sides A and B will be created (Figure 4.6). If the parameter is set to *false*, the normal 3D geometry is generated. Within the module *output* we switch between these two modes by using an if-statement. The expression `if (templates)` is an abbreviation of `if (templates == true)`. But how does our shelf bracket geometry get into the module *output*? This is done by the keyword *children*. With it we get access to the element following our module! The parameter `0` indicates that we want to have the first element. If our module would be followed by a geometry set enclosed in curly brackets (`{ ... }`), we could also access further elements. In this case, the special variable *$children* would tell us how many elements there are. In our case, however, we know that there is only one subsequent element (our shelf bracket). Thus, we do not need *$children* at this point.

In general, the *children* keyword allows us to define modules that behave like transformations. For the most time, one does not need this capability too often. However, there are situations where it can be used to achieve very elegant solutions for otherwise elaborate geometry descriptions.

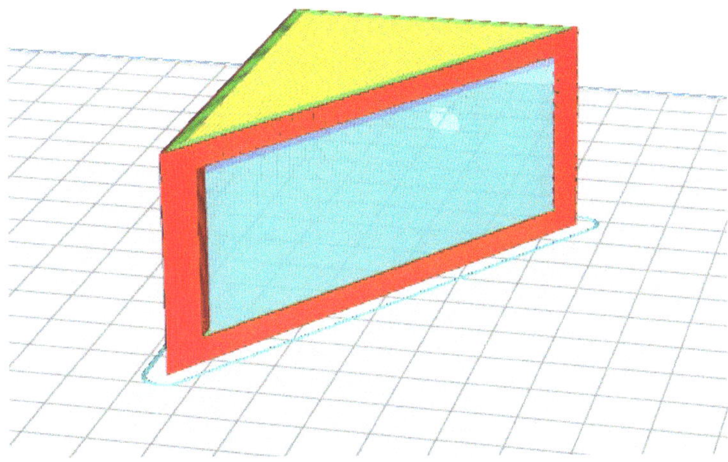

Figure 4.7: Shelf bracket in slicer software (here: Cura). Lying on its side, the component becomes stable but requires a support structure (blue).

4.4 3D printing tips

If we want to print our geometry with a 3D printer, we have to render our geometry first (*F6*). Depending on the complexity of the geometry, this can sometimes take a few minutes. Just be patient here. When the rendering is done, you can export the resulting geometry (*File -> Export -> Export as . . .*). A typical format is `.stl`. You can then load the `.stl` file into a so-called *slicer* software and prepare the geometry for 3D printing.

Within the slicer software, the question arises in which orientation one would like to print the shelf bracket. Since 3D-printed components are created in layers, the stability of the components within a layer is significantly greater than between the layers. In particular, shear forces acting on the layers can cause a component to break. For our shelf bracket, it would therefore be best to print it lying on its side. One disadvantage of this orientation is that you need a support structure within the component to stabilize the top-lying stringer during printing (Figure 4.7).

An alternative orientation, which may not require a support structure but still results in a stable part, is to print the bracket lying on the tapered side. Finding the right angle for this orientation directly in the slicer software can be a bit tricky. In this case it is easier to export the geometry already in the correct orientation from OpenSCAD. We can extend our module *shelf_bracket* once again to support this orientation:

```
module shelf_bracket( side_a, side_b, width, thickness, rotate_it = false ) {

    module xhole_plate(size, h_dm, h_num, margin) {
        /* ... */
    }

    diag  = sqrt( pow(side_a[0], 2) + pow(side_b[0], 2) );
    angle = asin( side_a[0] / diag );

    rotate( [0, rotate_it ? 90 + angle : 0, 0] )
    difference() {

        union() {

            // side A
            xhole_plate(
                /* ... */
            );

            // side B
            translate([thickness,0,0])
            rotate([0,-90,0])
            xhole_plate(
                /* ... */
            );

            // stringer
            cube( [side_a[0], thickness, side_b[0]] );

            translate( [0, width - thickness, 0] )
            cube( [side_a[0], thickness, side_b[0]] );
        }

        translate( [side_a[0], -1, 0] )
        rotate( [0, -angle, 0] )
        cube( [diag, width + 2, diag + 2] );
    }
}
```

We add to our module another parameter *rotate_it* and give it the default value *false*. Then we move the calculation of the diagonal and the angle upwards in front of the

Boolean difference and rotate the whole object around the Y-axis clockwise by '90 + angle' degrees if the parameter *rotate_it* is true. Otherwise we do not rotate (0 degrees).

If we now export our geometry again as `.stl` file, our part lies in the correct orientation for the slicer software and can be printed without a support structure but still as a strong object (Figure 4.8).

After you have printed the shelf bracket, it is advisable to measure all the dimensions of the printed object once. In particular, the holes may not have been printed true to size. If this is the case, you can now benefit from the power of parametric modeling. You can simply adjust the diameters accordingly in the shelf bracket parameters and have an adjusted geometry generated at the push of a button.

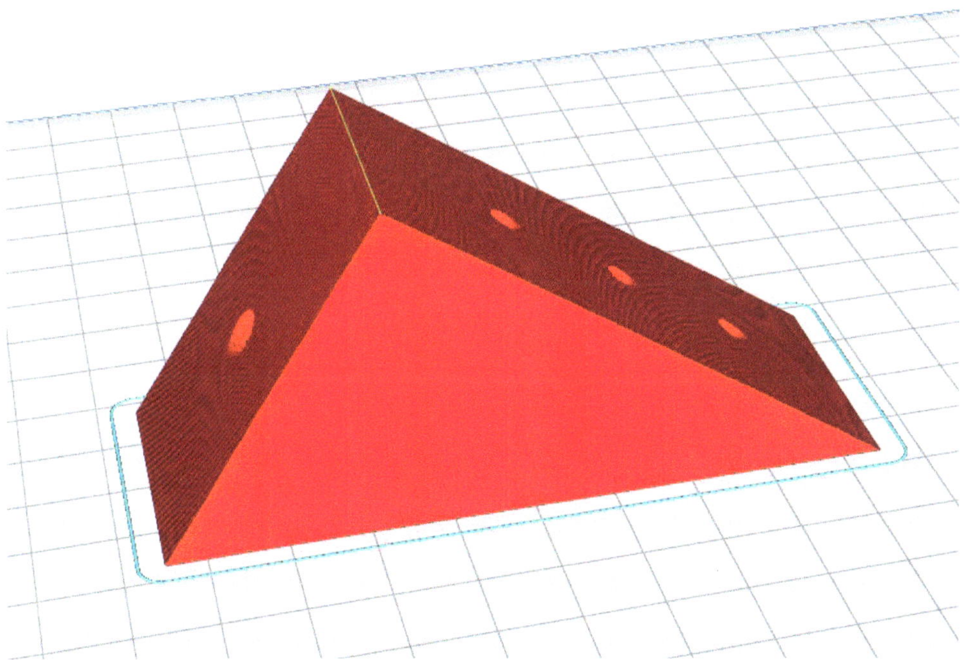

Figure 4.8: Shelf bracket in slicer software (here: Cura). Lying on the tapered side, the component also becomes strong, but does **not** need a support structure.

Project 2: Wall Anchor

If you live in an older house, you may know this problem. You want to hang something on the wall or ceiling, start to drill a hole and suddenly the drill starts to wander. You end up with a pretty big hole in the wall that is way too big for the screws you want to use. In this project we want to design a special wall anchor that can help you in this case.

5.1   What's new?

We will create our first *extrusion object* using the 2D basic shapes *square* and *circle* together with the linear extrusion transformation *linear_extrude*. Furthermore, we will get to know a new variant of the rotation transformation *rotate* as well as the 3D basic shape *cylinder*. Lastly, we will deepen our knowledge of already known functions.

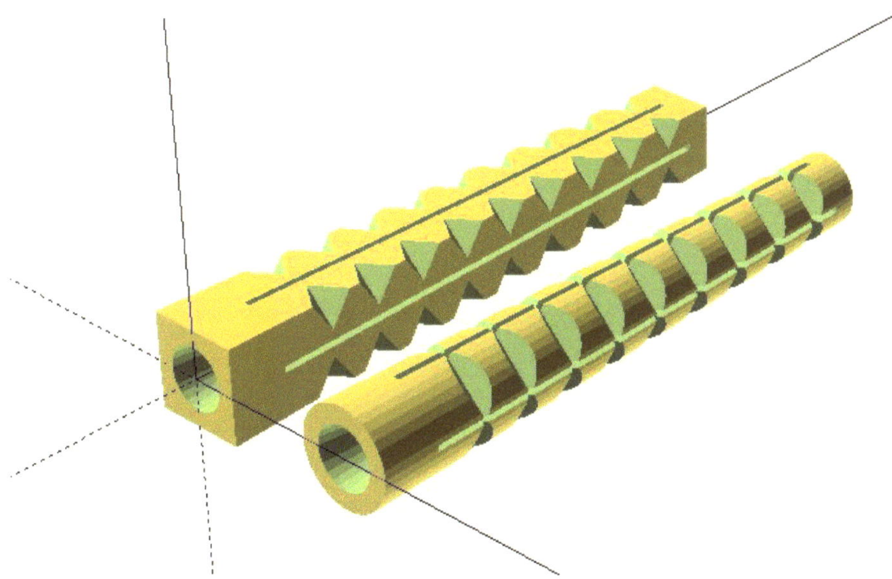

Figure 5.1: Wall anchor with square and round shape

5.2 Let's go

Again, let's start by first defining a module and a test instance of that module:

```
// a special wall anchor with lots of adjustments
// (all sizes in millimeter)

module wall_anchor (
    drill_hole_dm,          // drill hole diameter
    screw_dm,               // screw diameter
    length                  // anchor length
){

}

wall_anchor(8,5,50);
```

Since we are going to add quite a few parameters to our module, we arrange the parameters as a vertical list this time. This also allows us to add comments to the parameters right next to them. Let's begin with a square shaped wall anchor. We will add the round version of the anchor as an option later. If the wall anchor has a square cross-section and it has to fit into a round drill hole, then the diagonal of the square must correspond to the diameter of the drill hole. In order to derive the side length of the square from the diameter of the drill hole, old Pythagoras can help us again:

```
module wall_anchor (
    drill_hole_dm,          // drill hole diameter
    screw_dm,               // screw diameter
    length                  // anchor length
){

    side_length = sqrt( pow(drill_hole_dm, 2) / 2 );

    linear_extrude( height = length )
    square( side_length, center = true );
}
```

We know that $a^2 + b^2 = c^2$ holds true in a right triangle. In our particular case here, the long side of the triangle c is given and we are looking for the length of the small sides. Since our triangle is in a square, we already know that the small sides are equal in length. So we can rewrite our formula to $a^2 + a^2 = c^2$ or $2 \times a^2 = c^2$. If we now move the 2 to the other side of the equation, we are almost done: a^2 = c^2 / 2. To get *a*, we only have to take the square root: a = sqrt(c^2 / 2).

In this project we do not use the 3D basic shape *cube* to describe the body of the wall anchor. Instead, we use its two-dimensional counterpart *square* and then transform the 2D shape into a 3D object by using *linear_extrude*. We will see the benefit of this approach in the next step.

As mentioned above, our wall anchor should also work in "difficult" drill holes that have become larger than planned due to the drill wandering. Therefore, we want the basic shape of our anchor to be wedge-shaped. We add two new parameters that will allow us to adjust our wall anchor in this regard as needed. The parameter *oversize* will be added to the drill diameter. The parameter *outer_taper* is a taper factor that makes the wall anchor thinner towards the end. Instead of a factor one could also consider specifying a "target diameter". However, this would mean that you always have to specify this diameter, since it has to be selected to match the borehole diameter. Using a taper factor allows to give the parameter a reasonable default value that links the resulting taper to the borehole diameter. Thus, the parameter has to be changed only if this default value does not lead to a good result. As we implement the taper in our geometry description we can now benefit from our decision to use a combination of *square* and *linear_extrude* instead of using a *cube*:

```
module wall_anchor (
    drill_hole_dm,              // drill hole diameter
    screw_dm,                   // screw diameter
    length,                     // anchor length
    oversize        = 2,        // outer diameter oversize
    outer_taper     = 0.75, // outer taper factor
){

    outer_dm    = drill_hole_dm + oversize;
    side_length = sqrt( pow(outer_dm, 2) / 2 );

    linear_extrude( height = length, scale = outer_taper )
    square( side_length, center = true );
}
```

The transformation *linear_extrude* offers a parameter *scale*, with which we can reduce or enlarge the 2D shape along the extrusion path. So with the help of this parameter we can very easily describe the desired taper of the wall anchor. The parameter *oversize* is used in the calculation of *side_length*.

The cavity inside our wall anchor, i.e., the hole in which we screw in the screw, has the shape of a funnel. At the beginning, the hole in the anchor has the diameter of the screw. Then it tapers so that the screw can push the sides of the anchor apart and press them against the inside of the hole. We can make this funnel shape with two cylinders and subtract both from our main body using a Boolean difference operation:

```
module wall_anchor (
    drill_hole_dm,              // drill hole diameter
    screw_dm,                   // screw diameter
    length,                     // anchor length
    oversize        = 2,     // outer diameter oversize
    outer_taper     = 0.75, // outer taper factor
    inner_taper     = 0.2,  // inner taper factor
    inner_taper_end = 0.3,   // relative end of inner taper along length
){

    difference() {

        outer_dm    = drill_hole_dm + oversize;
        side_length = sqrt( pow(outer_dm, 2) / 2 );

        linear_extrude( height = length, scale = outer_taper )
        square( side_length, center = true );

        // hole
        abs_taper_end = length * inner_taper_end;
        taper_dm      = screw_dm * inner_taper;

        translate( [0, 0, -0.01] )
        union() {
            $fn = 24;

            cylinder( d1 = screw_dm, d2 = taper_dm, h = abs_taper_end + 0.01);

            translate( [0, 0, abs_taper_end] )
            cylinder( d = taper_dm, h = length - abs_taper_end + 0.02 );
        }
    }
}
```

We have added two more parameters to our module. The parameter *inner_taper* sets the taper factor of the inner diameter and determines how thin the neck of our funnel

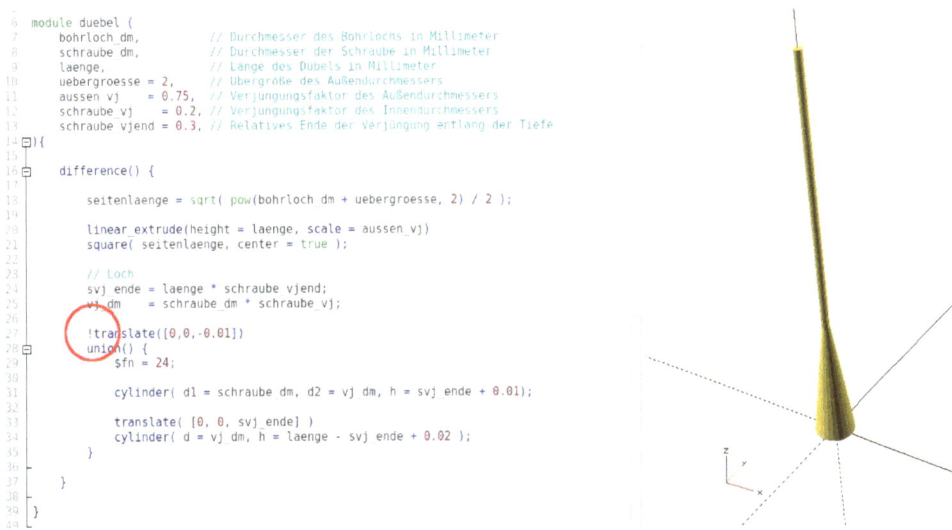

```
 6  module duebel (
 7      bohrloch_dm,           // Durchmesser des Bohrlochs in Millimeter
 8      schraube_dm,           // Durchmesser der Schraube in Millimeter
 9      laenge,                // Länge des Dübels in Millimeter
10      uebergroesse = 2,      // Übergröße des Außendurchmessers
11      aussen_vj    = 0.75,   // Verjüngungsfaktor des Außendurchmessers
12      schraube_vj    = 0.2,  // Verjüngungsfaktor des Innendurchmessers
13      schraube_vjend = 0.3,  // Relatives Ende der Verjüngung entlang der Tiefe
14  ){
15
16      difference() {
17
18          seitenlaenge = sqrt( pow(bohrloch_dm + uebergroesse, 2) / 2 );
19
20          linear_extrude(height = laenge, scale = aussen_vj)
21          square( seitenlaenge, center = true );
22
23          // Loch
24          svj_ende = laenge * schraube_vjend;
25          vj_dm    = schraube_dm * schraube_vj;
26
27          !translate([0,0,-0.01])
28          union() {
29              $fn = 24;
30
31              cylinder( d1 = schraube_dm, d2 = vj_dm, h = svj_ende + 0.01);
32
33              translate( [0, 0, svj_ende] )
34              cylinder( d = vj_dm, h = laenge - svj_ende + 0.02 );
35          }
36
37      }
38
39  }
```

Figure 5.2: Preview individual geometry parts by temporarily prefixing them with a ! character

shape becomes. The parameter *inner_taper_end* sets the position where the neck of our funnel shape starts. The position is specified relative to the *length* of the anchor. Inside the module, we made the definition of our wall anchor shape the first element of a Boolean difference operation. We then described our funnel shape as the second element of this operation in order to subtract it from the main body. For this we first derive the absolute values *abs_taper_end* and *taper_dm* from the relative parameters *inner_taper_end* and *inner_taper*. We then describe the funnel shape with two cylinders. The first cylinder uses a new form of parameterization. Instead of a diameter *d* we specify two diameters *d1* and *d2*. This creates a blunt cone with diameter *d1* at the bottom and diameter *d2* at the top. In our case we start with the screw diameter *screw_dm* and end with the diameter of the taper *taper_dm*. The height corresponds to the end of the taper *abs_taper_end* plus some allowance. The second cylinder is defined with just one diameter and describes the neck of our funnel shape. It has the diameter *taper_dm* and as height the remaining length of the anchor (`length - abs_taper_end`) plus some allowance. We combine both cylinders with a Boolean union and move the funnel shape minimally down so that the difference operation with the anchor main body performs cleanly.

A small side note: within the Boolean union, the first statement sets the special variable *$fn*, which we use to control the level of detail of our geometry. Since we want to increase the level of detail of both cylinders, we can simply set the variable *$fn* within the local geometry set of the Boolean operation. By doing so, we will affect all curved geometries inside the set.

Since our funnel shape is the subtractive part of a difference operation, it is somewhat difficult to model the shape "blindly". If we prefix the funnel shape with an exclamation mark (!translate(...) union() ...) and run a preview, then only the funnel shape will be drawn and no other geometry (Figure 5.2). This selective preview of individual geometry parts is very useful and you will probably use it very often as a modeling aid.

Our wall anchor is still missing the ability to expand when a screw is screwed in. To allow for such expansion, we slit the anchor on all four sides using cubes and the Boolean difference operation:

```
module wall_anchor (
    drill_hole_dm,              // drill hole diameter
    screw_dm,                   // screw diameter
    length,                     // anchor length
    oversize        = 2,        // outer diameter oversize
    outer_taper     = 0.75,     // outer taper factor
    inner_taper     = 0.2,      // inner taper factor
    inner_taper_end = 0.3,      // relative end of inner taper along length
    collar          = 0.1,      // relative length of initial non-slit part
    slit            = 0.5,      // slit width
    cap_size        = 2,        // length of the end cap
){
    difference() {

        outer_dm    = drill_hole_dm + oversize;
        side_length = sqrt( pow(outer_dm, 2) / 2 );

        /* .. */
        // slits
        abs_collar = length * collar;

        for (i = [0:1])
        rotate( [0, 0, i * 90] )
        translate( [-(side_length + 2) / 2, -slit / 2, abs_collar] )
        cube ( [side_length + 2, slit, length - cap_size - abs_collar] );
    }
}
```

```
34          cylinder( d1 = schraube_dm, d2 = vj_dm, h = svj_ende + 0.01);

36          translate( [0, 0, svj_ende] )
37          cylinder( d = vj_dm, h = laenge - svj_ende + 0.02 );
38      }

41      // Schlitze
42      kragen_abs = laenge * kragen;

44      #for (i = [0:1])
45      rotate( [0, 0, i * 90] )
46      translate([
47          -(seitenlaenge + 2) / 2,
48          -schlitzstaerke / 2,
49          kragen_abs
50      ])
51      cube ([
52          seitenlaenge + 2,
53          schlitzstaerke,
54          laenge - abschluss - kragen_abs
55      ]);

57  }
```

Figure 5.3: Highlighting individual geometry parts by temporarily prefixing them with a # character

We have added three more parameters to our model to control the slits in the wall anchor. The parameter *collar* defines how long the section should be at the beginning of the anchor where there are no slits. This length is given relative to the total length. The parameter *slit* defines the thickness of the slits in millimeters. The parameter *cap_size* determines how many millimeters before the end of the anchor the slits should end. Preventing the slits to go through the end of the wall anchor stabilizes the anchor. Within the module description, the slits are modeled using a box (*cube*). The box is translated such that it is centered above the origin of the X/Y plane at a Z-level of *abs_collar* and then rotated around the Z-axis. The rotation is parameterized by the loop variable *i*, which runs from 0 to 1. Thus, we create 2 instances of the box: one rotated by 0 degrees and one rotated by 90 degrees. To check the shape of these two boxes, you can make them temporarily visible by prefixing the for-loop with a # character and running a preview (Figure 5.3).

In order to be able to grip well in a drilled hole, we now want to give our wall anchor some teeth:

```
module wall_anchor (
    drill_hole_dm,              // drill hole diameter
    screw_dm,                   // screw diameter
    length,                     // anchor length
    oversize           = 2,     // outer diameter oversize
```

```
    outer_taper      = 0.75, // outer taper factor
    inner_taper      = 0.2,  // inner taper factor
    inner_taper_end = 0.3,  // relative end of inner taper along length
    collar           = 0.1,  // relative length of initial non-slit part
    slit             = 0.5,  // slit width
    cap_size         = 2,    // length of the end cap
    teeth_div        = 5,    // divisor determining the number of teeth
    teeth_depth      = 1.5,  // depth of the teeth
){

    difference() {

        outer_dm    = drill_hole_dm + oversize;
        side_length = sqrt( pow(outer_dm, 2) / 2 );

        /* .. */

        abs_collar = length * collar;

        /* .. */

        // teeth
        teeth_count = floor( (length - abs_collar) / teeth_div );
        teeth_dist  = (length - abs_collar) / (teeth_count + 1);

        opposite   = (outer_dm - (outer_dm * outer_taper)) / 2;
        hypotenuse = sqrt( pow(opposite, 2) + pow(length, 2) );
        angle      = asin( opposite / hypotenuse );

        diag_dist = sqrt( pow(outer_dm/2 - teeth_depth, 2) / 2 );

        for ( j = [0:90:359] )
        rotate( [0, 0, j] )
        rotate( -angle, [1,1,0] )
        for (i = [1:teeth_count] )
        translate( [diag_dist, -diag_dist, abs_collar + i * teeth_dist] )
        rotate([0,0,-45])
        translate( [0, -outer_dm / 2, 0] )
        rotate([0,45,0])
        cube( outer_dm );
    }
}
```

For the teeth we define two more parameters. The parameter *teeth_div* determines the number of teeth relative to the length of the wall anchor. The parameter *teeth_depth* defines how deep the teeth should penetrate into the main body of the anchor. Inside the module we first derive the absolute values *teeth_count* and *teeth_dist* from the parameter *teeth_div*. The length considered for the number of teeth is the length of the anchor minus the collar. The function *floor* used here rounds the value passed to it down to the nearest integer. The value *teeth_dist* is used to distribute the teeth evenly along the anchor. The number of teeth is increased by 1 in this context to gain some distance from the edge at both the beginning and the end of the anchor. Since our anchor tapers, we also need to determine the *angle* of the side edge using the arc sine. Lastly, we need the distance *diag_dist*, which gives us the displacement in X- and Y-direction that is needed to translate from the origin to the outer tip of the wall anchor base.

After these preparations, we can now describe the teeth geometry. Since our geometry description contains a whole series of steps, it is advisable to preview each step by placing a ! sign in front of the geometry description at corresponding positions. We start with a cube that has an edge length of *outer_dm*. If we put the ! sign directly in front of *cube* and run a preview (*F5*), only this cube will be displayed. In the next step we rotate the cube by 45 degrees along the Y-axis (`!rotate( [0, 45, 0] )`). This creates the "cutting face" along the Y-axis, which we will use later to cut into the base body. Now we center the cube over the X-axis by moving it half its length along the Y-axis (`!translate( [0, -outer_dm / 2, 0] )`). Now the cube is in a good position to be rotated around the Z-axis by -45 degrees (`!rotate([0,0,-45])`). The cube is almost in the right position. We only have to move it to the outer edge of the anchor base and a little bit upwards (`!translate( [diag_dist, -diag_dist, collar_abs + i * teeth_dist] )`). In this translate transformation we have already included the loop variable i. If we now put a for loop in front of it, we end up with a tower of cubes (`!for ( i = [1:teeth_count] )`).

We need to take care of the taper of our wall anchor now. Our cube tower should be tilted in such a way that it follows the side of the wall anchor's edge. For this we have to rotate the cube tower by *angle* degrees. However, we don't want to rotate around any of the coordinate axes, but around an axis that lies exactly between the X- and Y-axis. To achieve this we use a special form of the rotate transform. This special form receives the rotation angle as first parameter and the rotation axis as second parameter (`!rotate( -angle, [1,1,0])`).

We're almost there! Now we only have to copy our tilted cube tower three times, rotating it 90 degrees each time. We do this with another for-loop and a corresponding rotate transformation (`!for ( j = [0:90:359]) rotate( [0, 0, j] )`). The for-loop ends at 359 and not at 360, because otherwise we would have cube towers at 0 degrees and at 360 degrees lying on top of each other.

As a final touch, we want to give our special wall anchor the option of having a round base shape instead of a square one:

```openscad
module wall_anchor (
    drill_hole_dm,              // drill hole diameter
    screw_dm,                   // screw diameter
    length,                     // anchor length
    oversize        = 2,        // outer diameter oversize
    outer_taper     = 0.75,     // outer taper factor
    inner_taper     = 0.2,      // inner taper factor
    inner_taper_end = 0.3,      // relative end of inner taper along length
    collar          = 0.1,      // relative length of initial non-slit part
    slit            = 0.5,      // slit width
    cap_size        = 2,        // length of the end cap
    teeth_div       = 5,        // divisor determining the number of teeth
    teeth_depth     = 1.5,      // depth of the teeth
    round_shape     = false     // make the anchor round instead of square
){
    difference() {

        outer_dm = drill_hole_dm + oversize;
        side_length   =
            round_shape ? outer_dm : sqrt( pow(outer_dm, 2) / 2 );

        linear_extrude( height = length, scale = outer_taper )
        if ( round_shape )
            circle( d = side_length, $fn=36 );
        else
            square( side_length, center = true );

        // hole
        abs_taper_end = length * inner_taper_end;
        taper_dm      = screw_dm * inner_taper;

        translate( [0, 0, -0.01] )
        union() {
            $fn = 24;

            cylinder( d1 = screw_dm, d2 = taper_dm, h = abs_taper_end + 0.01);

            translate( [0, 0, abs_taper_end] )
            cylinder( d = taper_dm, h = length - abs_taper_end + 0.02 );
        }
```

```
        // slits
        abs_collar = length * collar;

        for (i = [0:1])
        rotate( [0, 0, i * 90] )
        translate([
            -(side_length + 2) / 2,
            -slit / 2,
            abs_collar
        ])
        cube ([
            side_length + 2,
            slit,
            length - cap_size - abs_collar
        ]);

        // teeth
        teeth_count = floor( (length - abs_collar) / teeth_div );
        teeth_dist  = (length - abs_collar) / (teeth_count + 1);

        opposite = (outer_dm - (outer_dm * outer_taper)) / 2;
        hypotenuse  = sqrt( pow(opposite, 2) + pow(length, 2) );
        angle = asin( opposite / hypotenuse );

        diag_dist = sqrt( pow(outer_dm/2 - teeth_depth, 2) / 2 );

        for ( j = [0:90:359] )
        rotate( [0, 0, j] )
        rotate( -angle, [1,1,0] )
        for (i = [1:teeth_count] )
        translate( [diag_dist, -diag_dist, abs_collar + i * teeth_dist] )
        rotate([0,0,-45])
        translate( [0, -outer_dm / 2, 0] )
        rotate([0,45,0])
        cube( outer_dm );

    }

}

wall_anchor(8,5,50);
```

The option to make the anchor round or square is controlled by the newly added parameter *round_shape*. Inside the geometry description we have extended two code locations with a case distinction. First, the *side_length* is set depending on the parameter *round_shape*. Second, we distinguish between circular and square basic shape by means of an if-branch. Note that here the if-branch itself is treated like a geometry that is then extruded by a *linear_extrude* transform.

Our finished wall anchor module has received quite a lot of parameters! However, by defining most of the parameters as relative parameters and giving them sensible default values, the module remains pretty usable. Only the three parameters *drill_hole_dm*, *screw_dm* and *length* have to be specified. Everything else adapts automatically in relation to these three parameters.

5.3   3D printing tips

After you have rendered the geometry (*F6*) and exported it as a `.stl` file (*F7*), you can load the `.stl` file into the *slicer* software of your 3D printer. Here, you have to decide if you want to print the anchor standing up or lying down. Lying down should make the anchor a bit more stable and it will require less printing time, but it will also require a support structure that you have to remove after printing. If you print the anchor upright, the need for a support structure is eliminated. In this case, you might want to reduce the printing speed a bit so that the individual layers have more time to cool down sufficiently before the next layer is applied. In addition, it could be advantageous to print with a so-called *brim* so that the contact area of the anchor on the print bed is increased and print bed adhesion is improved.

Project 3: Window Stopper

In this project we design a window stopper with a rotating wedge. If you turn the lever of the stopper, the wedge jams the window upwards and locks it in place.

6.1 What's new?

We will learn about a new variant of the for-loop (*generative for*), with which we can create function-based arrays. In this context we will also learn about the keyword *let* and see how we can transform the generated data into a geometry using the 2D basic form *polygon*. Last but not least, we will also learn what the *hull* transformation is all about.

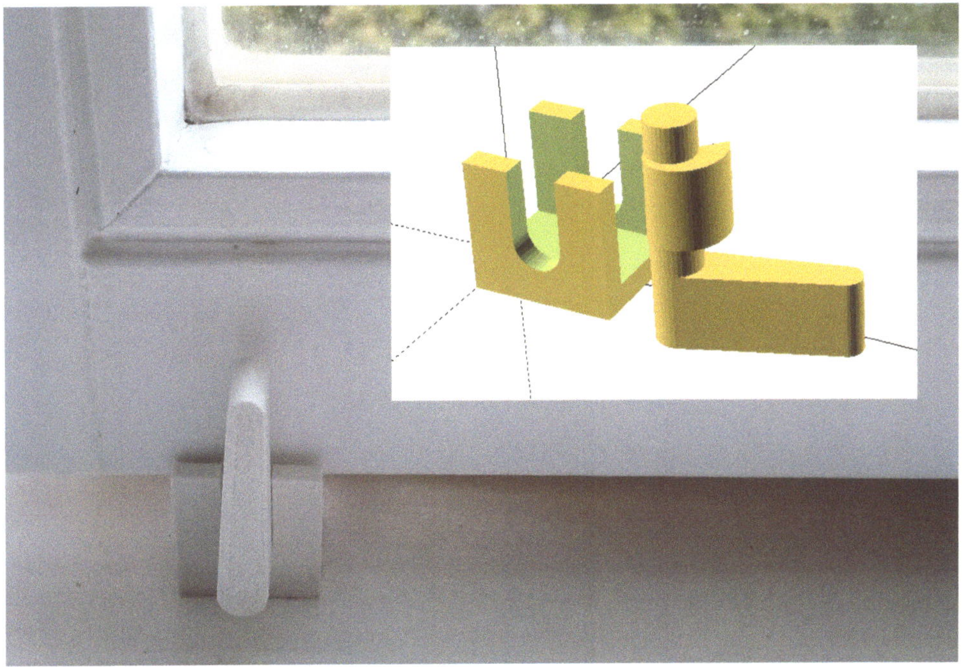

Figure 6.1: Window stopper with rotating wedge

6.2   Let's go

Let's start, as we are used to by now, with the definition of a module *window_stopper*.
Since we expect quite a number of parameters, we will choose a vertical parameter
arrangement again. Furthermore, we prepare some empty sub-modules to split our
geometry description into several parts:

```
// a window stopper with rotating wedge
// (all sizes in millimeter)

module window_stopper(

    /* parameters */

){

    $fn = 36;

    module window() {
    }

    module stopper_case() {
    }

    module stopper() {
    }

    window();
    stopper_case();
    stopper();

}

window_stopper(

    /* parameters */

);
```

Even though we will use each submodule only once, the subdivision into several submodules
will help us when we later want to generate the individual geometry parts, e.g. for a
3D print. The *window* module will be a purely auxiliary module, in which we model the
bottom edge of the window as an orientation guide. In the *stopper_case* module we will

describe the housing of the window stopper and in the *stopper* module we will define the rotating wedge as well as its lever. In addition to the submodules and their three instances, we defined the special variable *$fn* at the module level. This way we set the level of detail of all curved geometries in our module.

Let's start our geometry description with the auxiliary module *window*:

```
module window_stopper(
    window_thickness,          // thickness of window frame
    windowsill_dist,           // distance between window and windowsill
){
    $fn = 36;

    module window() {
        color("LightSkyBlue")
        translate( [-20, -window_thickness / 2, windowsill_dist] )
        cube( [100, window_thickness, 0.1] );
    }
    /* ... */
}
```

We have added the parameters *window_thickness* and *windowsill_dist* to our module. They describe the thickness of the window and the distance of the lower edge of the window to the window sill. In the submodule *window* we only describe this lower edge of the window with a 0.1 millimeter thin box (*cube*). We set the width of the cube to an arbitrary 10cm, as this dimension is not relevant for the construction of the stopper. Using the translation transform we bring the cube to the height *windowsill_dist* and center it over the x-axis (`-windowsill depth / 2`). To visually set off our auxiliary object from the rest of the geometry, we give it a nice shade of blue. Since we use the submodule only once and do not need to parameterize it, the parameter list is empty. We can access the parameters of the parent module *window_stopper* directly and do not have to pass them on using local parameters. This also applies to variables defined in the parent module. We will take advantage of this in the next step.

The geometry description of the holder is a bit more involved. In essence, however, the holder consists only of a simple box (*cube*), from which we subtract a series of suitably rotated and displaced basic shapes (*cube* and *cylinder*) using a Boolean difference operation:

```openscad
module window_stopper(
    window_thickness,           // thickness of window frame
    windowsill_dist,            // distance between window and windowsill
    windowsill_adj     = 0,     // adjustment for windowsill distance
    stopper_width      = 30,    // width of the stopper
    material_thickness = 5,     // material thickness of the stopper
    window_overlap     = 7,     // overlap of stopper and window
    axle_dm            = 10,    // axle diameter
    axle_clearance     = 0.5,   // axle clearance towards bushing
){
    $fn = 36;
    axle_height =
        material_thickness + (windowsill_dist - material_thickness) / 2;

    /* ... */

    module stopper_case() {
        case_size = [
            stopper_width,
            window_thickness + 2 * material_thickness,
            windowsill_dist + window_overlap
        ];

        translate( [0, -case_size.y / 2, 0] )
        difference() {
            cube( case_size );

            translate( [-1, material_thickness, material_thickness] )
            cube( [case_size.x + 2, window_thickness, case_size.z] );

            axle_bushing = axle_dm + axle_clearance;

            translate( [case_size.x / 2, -1, axle_height] )
            rotate( [-90, 0, 0] )
            cylinder( d = axle_bushing, h = case_size.y + 2);

            translate( [(case_size.x - axle_bushing) / 2, -1, axle_height] )
            cube( [axle_bushing, case_size.y + 2, case_size.z] );
        }

        translate( [0, -case_size.y / 2, -windowsill_adj] )
        cube( [case_size.x, case_size.y, windowsill_adj] );
    }
    /* ... */
}
```

Our parameter list got a lot of new members. The parameter *windowsill_adj* allows a later readjustment of the window stopper. The parameters *stopper width* and *material thickness* define the width of the stopper case and the material thickness of the sides and the bottom of the case. The parameter *window_overlap* defines how far the stopper case should overlap laterally with the window. The parameters *axis_dm* and *axis_clearance* define the diameter of the axis of the rotating wedge and the size of the gap between the axis and its bearing in the stopper case.

Inside of the module *window stopper* we define the variable *axis_height* at a module-wide level. We will use the variable in both the submodule *stopper_case* and in the submodule *stopper*. We position the axis halfway between the window sill and the lower edge of the window, taking the material thickness of the stopper case into account. In the submodule *stopper_case* we define the variable *case_size*, which describes the dimension of our case as a three-dimensional vector that depends on window dimensions, material thickness and window overlap.

We describe the geometry of the stopper case via a Boolean difference operation. The main body, from which we subtract the other geometries, is a simple box. It has the outer dimensions of the stopper case (`cube( case_size );`). Subsequently, we subtract a box that has a depth matching that of the window and that is slightly wider than our main body (`case_size.x + 2`). We position the box upwards as well as inwards by the material thickness using a translate transformation. This turns the basic body into a U-profile that can later be moved along the window edge during operation of the stopper. Note the small displacement in the X direction (−1) to ensure a clean difference operation.

Next, we have to subtract the axle bearing from our stopper case. Since the bearing should be slightly larger in diameter than the axle itself, we define the variable *axle_bushing* as the sum of axle diameter and axle clearance. The axle bearing consists of a cylinder and a box (*cube*). The cylinder gets the diameter *axle_bushing* and a height equal to the depth of the cube plus a small allowance. Since the basic shape *cylinder* starts out perpendicular to the X-Y plane, we first have to rotate the cylinder around the X-axis onto its side. Afterwards we can move the cylinder by means of *translate* to the center of the case width (`case_size.x / 2`) and the *axis_height* defined earlier. Corresponding to the allowance in cylinder height, we perform a small translation (−1) in the Y direction to ensure a clean difference operation. The second part of the axle bearing consists of a box, which is as wide as the cylinder (*axle_bushing*) and is cut above the axle from the stopper case. Since the basic shape *cube* was created without *center = true*, we have to consider its width when moving the box to the center of the stopper case (`(case_size.x - axle_bushing) / 2`). Apart from this, the positioning of the box is analogous to that of the cylinder before. Again we take care that the difference operation can run cleanly (allowance in depth and corresponding displacement).

Now that we have completed the stopper case description inside the Boolean difference operation, the last remaining step is to center the case on the X-axis by prefixing the difference operation with a corresponding translation.

In order to be able to readjust the distance between the window sill and the window in another, simpler way, we define a base outside of the difference operation that can grow below the stopper case if necessary (parameter *windowsill_adj*). This base consists of a simple box (*cube*), which has the base area of the stopper case and is *windowsill_adj* high. To make it "grow" downwards, we use a translate transform to move it by -*windowsill_adj* along the Z-axis. With the same transformation we also center the base on the X-axis (`-case_size.y / 2`);

We have finished the submodule *stopper_case* and can now turn to the submodule *stopper*. Since the module uses a number of new OpenSCAD functions, we want to proceed step by step:

```
module window_stopper(
    window_thickness,              // thickness of window frame
    windowsill_dist,               // distance between window and windowsill
    windowsill_adj      = 0,    // adjustment for windowsill distance
    stopper_width       = 30,   // width of the stopper
    material_thickness  = 5,    // material thickness of the stopper
    window_overlap      = 7,    // overlap of stopper and window
    axle_dm             = 10,   // axle diameter
    axle_clearance      = 0.5,  // axle clearance towards bushing
    wedge_start_r       = 0,    // wedge start radius
    wedge_end_r         = 11,   // wedge end radius
    wedge_angle         = 42,   // start angle of wedge
    lever_depth         = 15,   // depth of lever
    lever_length        = 40,   // length of lever
    lever_angle         = 15,   // start angle of lever
){
```

```
    $fn = 36;
    axle_height =
        material_thickness + (windowsill_dist - material_thickness) / 2;

    /* ... */

    module stopper( angle = 0 ) {
        axle_length = window_thickness + 2 * material_thickness + 2;

        translate( [stopper_width / 2, -axle_length / 2, axle_height] )
        rotate( [-90, 0, 0] )
        cylinder( d = axle_dm, h = axle_length );

        /* ... */
    }
    /* ... */
}
```

For the stopper we have defined another set of parameters. The three parameters *wedge_start_r*, *wedge_end_r* and *wedge_angle* specify properties of the rotating wedge. The parameters *lever_depth*, *lever_length* and *lever_angle* are associated with the stopper lever that will turn the rotating wedge. As we did in the *stopper_case* module, we will also use the variable *axis_height* in this submodule. In addition, we have defined the variable *axis_length* inside the *stopper* submodule. It corresponds to the width of the case plus two millimeters, making the axle protrude one millimeter (front and back) from the stopper case. The axle itself is modeled using the basic shape *cylinder* and moved to the correct position using rotate and translate transformations. The submodule *stopper* also has a parameter *angle*, which we will use later to test the function of the rotating wedge.

Next, we will model the rotating wedge, which will become part of the axle. To this end, we will first use a special variant of the for-loop to create an array of 2D points that describe the shape of the rotating wedge in two dimensions. Then we pass this set of points to the 2D basic shape *polygon*, which creates a 2D geometry from the set of points. We can then extrude this geometry using *linear_extrude* and move it to the desired location using the usual rotate and translate transformations:

```openscad
module window_stopper(
    /* ... */
){
    $fn = 36;
    axle_height =
        material_thickness + (windowsill_dist - material_thickness) / 2;

    /* ... */

    module stopper( angle = 0 ) {
        axle_length = window_thickness + 2 * material_thickness + 2;

        translate( [stopper_width / 2, -axle_length / 2, axle_height] )
        rotate( [-90, 0, 0] )
        cylinder( d = axle_dm, h = axle_length );

        points = [
            for (i = [0:5:360])
            let (
                radius = wedge_start_r + (wedge_end_r - wedge_start_r) * i / 360
            )
            [ cos( i ) * radius, sin( i ) * radius ]
        ];

        wedge_width = window_thickness - 2;

        translate( [stopper_width / 2, -wedge_width / 2, axle_height] )
        rotate( [-90, 0, 0] )
        rotate( [0, 0, wedge_angle + angle] )
        linear_extrude( height = wedge_width )
        polygon(points);

        /* ... */
    }
    /* ... */
}
```

The central element in the geometry description above is the variable *points*, to which
we assign an array (`points = [ ... ];`). The goal is to pass this array as a parameter
to the 2D basic shape *polygon*. The 2D base shape *polygon* expects an array of 2D
points or two-dimensional vectors:

```
    points = [ [x0,y0], [x1,y1], ..., [xN,yN] ];

    polygon( points );
```

It's easy to lose track with all those square brackets. The "outer" array consists of the square bracket at the very beginning and the one at the very end. Then inside, separated by commas, are the individual two-dimensional vectors with their x and y values. For simple 2D shapes, you could define such a set of points by hand or have them generated by an external program.

For our rotating wedge, we take a different approach and use a generative for-loop:

```
    points = [
        for (i = [0:5:360])
        let ( radius = wedge_start_r + (wedge_end_r - wedge_start_r) * i / 360 )
        [ cos( i ) * radius, sin( i ) * radius ]
    ];
```

The first line of the expression is similar to that of a regular for-loop. We define the loop variable *i* and assign it a range running from 0 to 360 in steps of 5 (`for (i = [0:5:360])`). The next line contains something new. The OpenSCAD expression `let( ... )` allows us to define one or more variables which are set anew in each loop iteration, just like it happens with the loop variable itself. In our case, we define the variable *radius* and give it a value that increases steadily as the loop progresses. This way, *radius* has the value *wedge_start_r* at the beginning of the loop and the value *wedge_end_r* at the end of the loop. The formula can be described roughly like this: we start with *wedge_start_r* and want to end up at *wedge_end_r*. The difference or the distance between *wedge_end_r* and *wedge_start_r* is `(wedge_end_r - wedge_start_r)`. To approach the value of *wedge_end_r* step by step, we need only a fraction of this distance (`i / 360`) in each step. When *i* has reached 360, our fraction is `360 / 360`, i.e. 1. Before that, *i* is smaller than 360 and thus results in a value smaller than 1 for the respective intermediate steps.

So now we have a variable *radius*, which becomes increasingly larger. Where do our points come from? We find them in the third line of our generative for-loop (`[ cos( i ) * radius, sin( i ) * radius ]`). The third line is a template of a single array entry. In our case we want this to be a two-dimensional vector (`[ .. , .. ]`). The

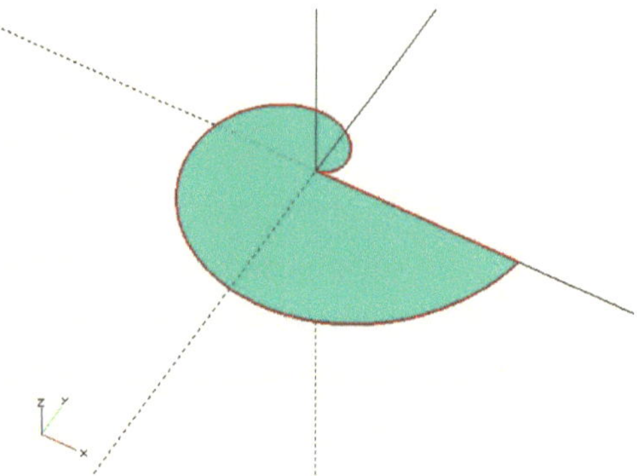

Figure 6.2: The 2D basic shape *polygon* enables the creation of formula-based geometries

x-value of the vector is `cos( i )` * `radius` and the y-value is `sin( i )` * `radius`. So here we use both the loop variable *i* and the variable *radius* defined with *let*. For each step of the for-loop, this template vector is filled with the current values of *i* and *radius*, and is then added to the array. If you want to have a look at the generated array, you can insert the OpenSCAD command `echo( points );` below (e.g.) the definition of *points* and run a preview (*F5*). The content of points will then be output in the console window of OpenSCAD.

If you now pass the variable *points* as a parameter to the 2D basic shape *polygon*, the passed set of points defines a two-dimensional geometry (Figure 6.2). We can then use this geometry like any other basic two-dimensional shape. To describe our rotating wedge, we extrude the shape using *linear_extrude* to a length of *wedge_width*, which we derived from *window_depth*. Next, we perform a rotation around the Z-axis (`rotate( [0, 0, wedge_angle + angle] )`). This rotation serves two purposes. First, we need to make sure that our wedge does not collide with the stopper case. For this, we need to find a suitable value for *wedge_angle* (Figure 6.3). Second, we rotate by the *angle* parameter to test the functionality of our rotating wedge later. Thus we combine both angles with an addition.

We perform a second rotation around the X-axis to get the rotating wedge horizontal and then move it to the appropriate location using a translate transformation.

Having finished the rotating wedge we can now turn to modeling the lever as last part of the *stopper* submodule. Here we will get to know the *hull* transformation:

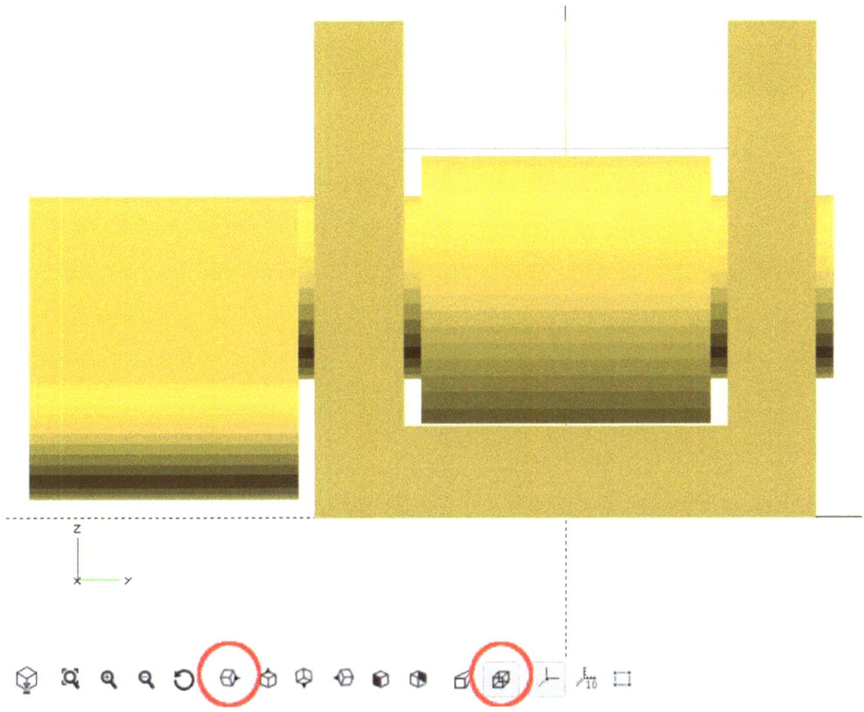

Figure 6.3: The orthogonal view (right marked button) can be helpful for fine tuning as there is no perspective distortion in this view. The figure shows a view from the right (left marked button) on the rotating wedge.

```
module window_stopper(
    /* ... */
){
    $fn = 36;
    axle_height =
        material_thickness + (windowsill_dist - material_thickness) / 2;


    /* ... */

    module stopper( angle = 0 ) {
        axle_length = window_thickness + 2 * material_thickness + 2;

        translate( [stopper_width / 2, -axle_length / 2, axle_height] )
        rotate( [-90, 0, 0] )
        cylinder( d = axle_dm, h = axle_length );
```

```
        points = [
            for (i = [0:5:360])
            let (
                radius = wedge_start_r + (wedge_end_r - wedge_start_r) * i / 360
            )
            [ cos( i ) * radius, sin( i ) * radius ]
        ];

        wedge_width = window_thickness - 2;

        translate( [stopper_width / 2, -wedge_width / 2, axle_height] )
        rotate( [-90, 0, 0] )
        rotate( [0, 0, wedge_angle + angle] )
        linear_extrude( height = wedge_width )
        polygon(points);

        translate( [stopper_width / 2, -axle_length / 2 + 0.1, axle_height] )
        rotate( [0, lever_angle + angle, 0] )
        rotate( [90, 0, 0] )
        linear_extrude( height = lever_depth )
        hull() {
            circle( d = axle_dm );
            translate( [lever_length - axle_dm / 2 - axle_dm / 3, 0, 0] )
            circle( d = axle_dm * 0.66 );
        }
    }
    /* ... */
}
```

The *hull* transformation acts similarly to Boolean operations on a geometry set ({ ... }). The transformation generates the joint convex hull over the geometries contained in the set (Figure 6.4). The *hull* transformation can be applied to both 2D and 3D geometries.

For the description of the lever we use the 2D version and generate the convex hull of two circles. We extrude the resulting basic shape of the lever using *linear_ extrude* and rotate the whole thing around the x-axis (`rotate( [90, 0, 0] )`). If we prepend a ! sign to the rotate transformation and run a preview (*F5*), we see that the Y-axis passes exactly through the center of rotation of the lever. We can now use a second rotate transformation (`rotate( [0, lever_angle + angle, 0] )`) to rotate the lever to its initial position, which is determined by the parameter *lever_ angle*. As with the rotating wedge, we also rotate by the test parameter *angle*. This way, the rotating wedge and the lever will turn together when we test the function of the stopper using the parameter

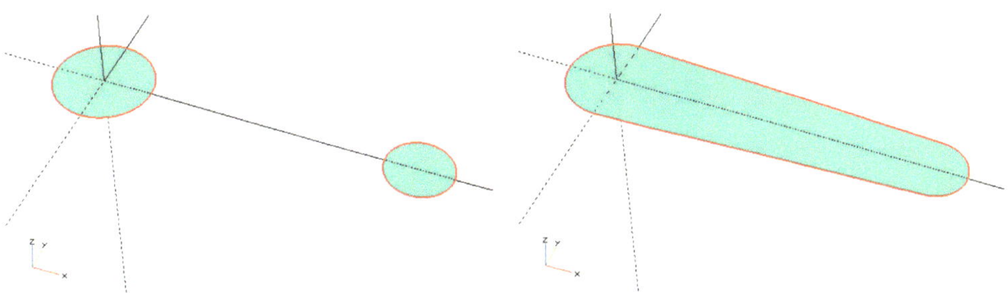

Figure 6.4: The *hull* transformation creates the convex hull (right) of the geometry set passed to it (left)

angle. We complete the geometry description of the lever by moving it to the appropriate position using a translate transformation. Note the slight addition of 0.1 along the Y-axis to ensure that lever and axle are connected.

We did it. The geometry description for our window stopper is complete! At this point, we should test whether the rotating wedge will actually press under the window. We can check this by turning lever and rotating wedge by 100 degrees counterclockwise with our test parameter *angle* of the stopper module:

```
/* ... */
module window_stopper(
    /* ... */
){

    /* ... */

    window();
    stopper_case();
    stopper( - 100);

}
/* ... */
```

If everything went right, the rotating wedge should now penetrate through the blue box of the window's bottom edge (after running a preview (*F5*)).

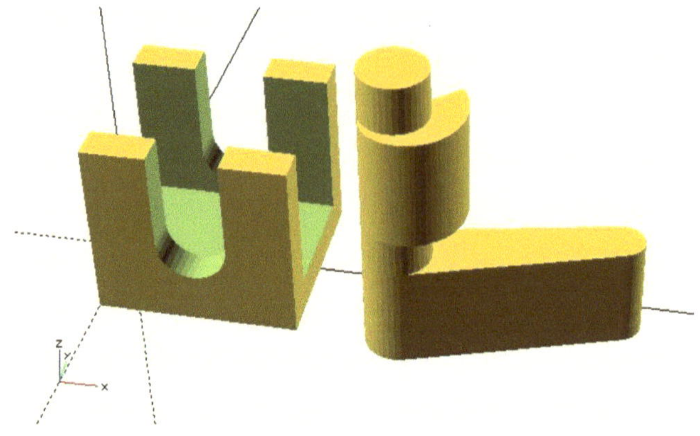

Figure 6.5: Print version of the window stopper geometry

6.3 3D printing tips

To print our window stopper, we need to have the *stopper_case* and *stopper* submodules rendered separately. The easiest way to do this is to temporarily prepend a ! character in front of the respective module instance. If we then trigger a render (*F6*), we can export the single geometry created in this way as a `.stl` file (*F7*).

Alternatively, the module *window_stopper* can be extended by a parameter *print_version* and a corresponding repositioning of the modules *stopper_case* and *stopper* by means of an if-statement:

```
module window_stopper(
    /* ... */
    print_version           = false
){
    /* ... */
    if (print_version) {
        stopper_case();

        translate([
            stopper_width,
            0,
            (window_thickness + 2 * material_thickness + 2) / 2 +
                lever_depth - 0.1
        ])
        rotate( [90, 0, 0] )
        stopper();
```

```
    } else {
        window();
        stopper_case();
        stopper( - 100);
    }
}
```

If *print_version* is true we rotate the *stopper* module to a suitable print orientation and translate it in a way that aligns the footpoints of *stopper_case* and *stopper* to the same height. In addition we make sure that the geometries do not overlap (Figure 6.5).

Project 4: Clock Movement Mockup

When designing a technical system, it regularly happens that already existing components have to be integrated. In the context of 3D printing, these are often motors, ball bearings, screws or nuts, for example. In such cases, it is helpful to measure and remodel these components and use them as mockups in the geometry description. This way, you can already see in the computer model whether all parts of the system really fit and are in the right place. If you use certain components frequently, it is worth storing them in an OpenSCAD library and then including them in the respective project using *include* or *use*.

In this project we want to take a closer look at important aspects that have to be considered if we want to create a useful OpenSCAD library. As example, we will remodel a standard clock movement and design the geometry description in such a way that it can be comfortably used as part of an OpenSCAD library.

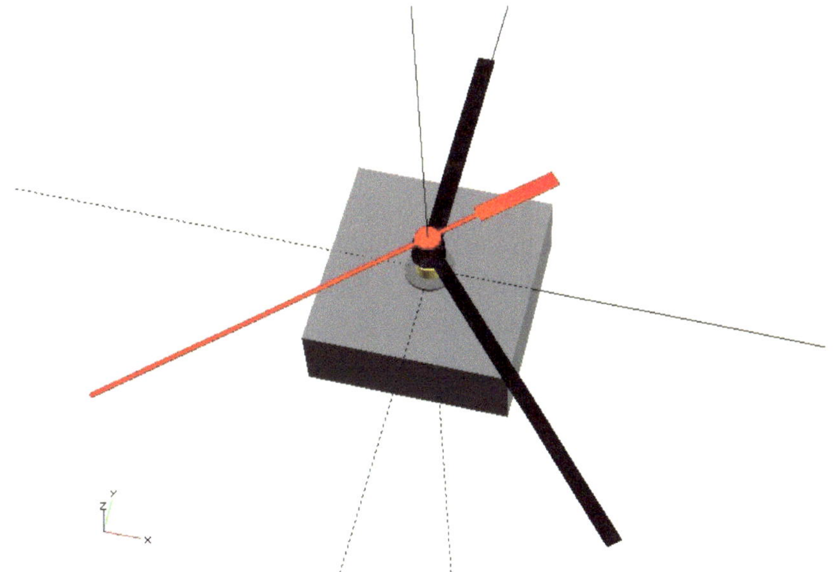

Figure 7.1: A remodeled clock movement as a mockup

7.1   What's new?

We will learn about the 2D basic shape *import* as well as the 3D basic shape *surface*. In terms of new transformations we will use *mirror* and *resize*. Furthermore we will use the *search* function and learn how to create simple animations with OpenSCAD.

7.2   Let's go

We start by defining a module and describing the box-shaped main body of the movement:

```
module clock_movement() {

    width  = 56;
    depth  = 56;
    height = 20;

    // main body
    color("Gray")
    translate( [-width / 2, -depth / 2, -height] )
    cube( [width, depth, height] );
}

clock_movement();
```

Since we are modeling a given physical object, we can assume the measured quantities to be fixed and therefore do not need to make them parameters of the module. Instead, we define them as variables within the module. Even though our geometry description is not very extensive so far, we have already made an important design decision. We decided to align the main body of the clock to the origin of the coordinate system in such a way that the surface of the main body is planar with the X-Y plane (displacement along the Z-axis by -height) and that later the axes of the clock movement will coincide with the Z-axis (displacement in X and Y direction by -width / 2 and -depth / 2). This alignment will not only simplify the following modeling steps, but will also improve the usability of the *clock_movement* module as part of an OpenSCAD library.

Surrounding the main axis of the movement, an alignment pattern protrudes from the main body. It consists of a flattened, notched cylinder. This alignment pattern serves to lock and align the movement when it is installed in a clock. It is therefore an important detail that should be present in our movement mockup:

```openscad
module clock_movement() {

    /* ... */
    alignment_dm        = 14; // diameter of alignment pattern
    alignment_h         = 1;  // height of alignment pattern
    alignment_flat      = 1;  // recess of flattening
    alignment_notch_dm = 6;   // diameter of alignment notches
    alignment_notch_fl = 2;   // recess of notch flattening


    /* ... */
    // alignment pattern
    difference(){
        color("DimGray")
        cylinder( d = alignment_dm, h = alignment_h, $fn = 36);


        // flattening and notch
        color("Gray")
        for ( i = [0:1])
        mirror( [i, 0, 0] )
        union(){
            translate([
                alignment_dm / 2 - alignment_flat,
                -(alignment_dm + 2) / 2,
                -1
            ])
            cube([
                alignment_flat + 1,
                alignment_dm + 2,
                alignment_h + 2
            ]);

            translate([
                alignment_dm / 2 - alignment_notch_fl +
                    alignment_notch_dm / 2,
                0,
                -1
            ])
            cylinder(
                d = alignment_notch_dm,
                h = alignment_h + 2,
                $fn = 18
            );
        }
    }
}
```

We describe the alignment pattern using the basic shape cylinder, from which we subtract the flattening and notches using a Boolean difference operation. We first model the flattening and notch on one side of the main cylinder by combining a box (*cube*) and a cylinder using a Boolean union. We position both geometries according to their respective setbacks and ensure sufficient allowances in dimensioning (and positioning) to ensure a clean difference operation.

Since our model is symmetric with respect to the origin, we can describe the flattening and notch on the other side of the main cylinder by a combination of mirror transformation and for-loop. The parameter of the mirror transformation is a three-dimensional vector that specifies along which axis we want to mirror our geometry. If the vector is the null vector ([0, 0, 0]), no mirroring takes place. Since our loop variable i becomes 0 and 1 exactly once, we thus create both our original flattening-notch pair and the mirrored pair on the opposite side.

If the movement is installed in a clock, it is fastened via a central screw terminal. Potential clocks must therefore have an appropriate hole that can receive that screw. We will only model this screw terminal as a simple cylinder and will not include the fine thread in our model:

```
module clock_movement() {

    /* ... */

    screw_terminal_dm = 7.8; // screw terminal diameter
    screw_terminal_h  = 5;   // screw terminal height
                             // measured from main body

    /* ... */

    // screw terminal
    color("Gold")
    cylinder( d = screw_terminal_dm, h = screw_terminal_h, $fn = 36);

}
```

The only thing missing from our geometry of the movement are the three axes for the hour, minute and second hands:

```
module clock_movement() {

    /* ... */

    hour_axle_dm = 5.1; // hour axle diameter
    hour_axle_h  = 8.3; // hour axle height

    minute_axle_dm = 3.2;  // minute axle diameter
    minute_axle_h  = 12.1; // minute axle height

    second_axle_dm = 1;    // second axle diameter
    second_axle_h  = 14.5; // second axle height

    /* ... */

    // axles
    color("Black") {
        cylinder( d = hour_axle_dm,   h = hour_axle_h,   $fn = 36);
        cylinder( d = minute_axle_dm, h = minute_axle_h, $fn = 36);
        cylinder( d = second_axle_dm, h = second_axle_h, $fn = 18);
    }
}
```

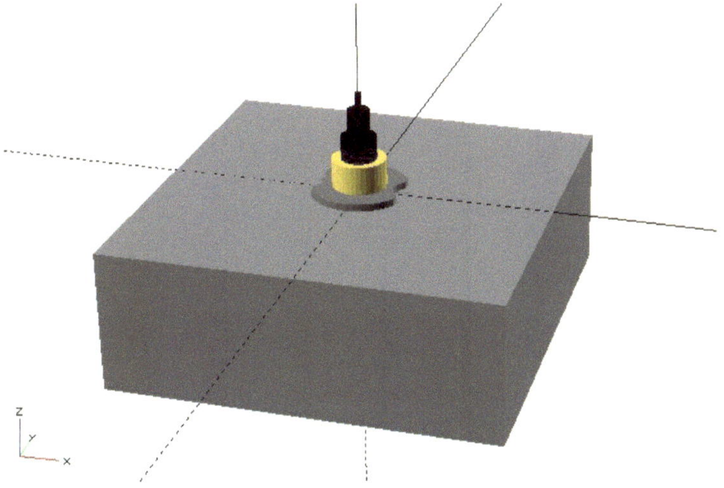

Figure 7.2: The finished clock movement model

Like the screw terminal, we model the axes as simple cylinders. A small side note: the use of the color transformation (`color("Black")`) here is an example that transformations can also be applied to geometry sets (`{ ... }`).

We could now already use our remodeled clock movement as a mockup object when designing a clock (Figure 7.2). For the design of a clock, however, it would be much more convenient if our model also had a set of hands. This would allow us to see right away, for example, whether the dial has the correct proportions. So let's give our clockwork model a set of hands:

```
module clock_movement( time = [12, 0, 0] ) {

    /* ... */

    // hands
    rotate( [0, 0, -360 * time[0] / 12] )
    translate( [0, 0, hour_axle_h - 1] )
    hour_hand();

    rotate( [0, 0, -360 * time[1] / 60] )
    translate( [0, 0, minute_axle_h - 1] )
    minute_hand();

    rotate( [0, 0, -360 * time[2] / 60] )
    translate( [0, 0, second_axle_h ] )
    second_hand();

    module hour_hand( ) {

        h = 0.4;    // height
        l = 72.35; // length
        r = 67.6;   // radius
        b = 5;      // width
        dm = 9.5;   // diameter

        color("Black")
        union() {
            cylinder( d = dm, h = h, $fn = 36 );

            translate( [-b / 2, 0, 0] )
            cube( [b, r, h] );
        }
    }
}
```

```
    module minute_hand() {

        h  = 0.4;   // height
        l  = 100.5; // length
        r  = 96;    // radius
        b  = 4;     // width
        dm = 9;     // diameter

        color("Black")
        union() {
            cylinder( d = dm, h = h, $fn = 36 );

            translate( [-b / 2, 0, 0] )
            cube( [b, r, h] );
        }
    }

    module second_hand() {

        b1  = 1.25; // width front part
        l1  = 95;   // length front part
        b2  = 1.25; // width neck
        l2  = 15;   // length neck
        b3  = 4.6;  // width back part
        l3  = 24;   // length back part
        dm  = 7.1;  // diameter
        h   = 0.4;  // material thickness

        color("Red")
        union() {
            cylinder( d = dm, h = h, $fn = 36);

            translate( [-b1 / 2, 0, 0] )
            cube( [b1, l1, h] );

            translate( [-b2 / 2, -l2, 0] )
            cube( [b2, l2, h] );

            translate( [-b3 / 2, -(l2 + l3), 0] )
            cube( [b3, l3, h] );
        }
    }
}
```

We have given our module *clock_movement* a parameter *time*, which expects a test time as a three-dimensional vector with [hours, minutes, seconds]. For each hand

Figure 7.3: Hands drawn as SVG can be loaded as geometry

we defined a separate submodule, so that we can simply move the respective hand geometries to the appropriate height and rotate them around the Z-axis according to *time*. To do this we convert the respective time data into corresponding angles.

The individual hands were measured, and the measured values were stored in variables within the submodules. The hands were then modeled using a combination of basic 3D shapes. Although the hands have a relatively simple shape (Figure 7.1), this procedure is relatively time consuming and results in a convoluted geometry description.

Since it is quite common for a clock movement to be sold with a selection of different hand styles, the previous approach is not particularly effective. An alternative way to modeling the hands consists in drawing the hands in an external drawing program and saving them as a .svg file (Figure 7.3). Using the *import* function of OpenSCAD such external drawings can then be loaded as a 2D basic shape:

```
module clock_movement( time = [12, 0, 0], hand_style = "modern") {

    /* ... */
    module hour_hand() {

        h = 0.4;    // height
        l = 72.35; // length
        r = 67.6;  // radius
        b = 5;      // width
        dm = 9.5;  // diameter

        if (hand_style == "modern") { /* ... */ }

        if (hand_style == "deco") {
            color("Black")
            linear_extrude(height = h)
            import("stunden.svg");
        }
    }
}
```

```
module minute_hand() {

    h  = 0.4;    // height
    l  = 100.5;  // length
    r  = 96;     // radius
    b  = 4;      // width
    dm = 9;      // diameter

    if (hand_style == "modern") { /* ... */ }

    if (hand_style == "deco") {
        color("Black")
        linear_extrude(height = h)
        import("minuten.svg");
    }
}

module second_hand() {

    b1  = 1.25; // width front part
    l1  = 95;   // length front part
    b2  = 1.25; // width neck
    l2  = 15;   // length neck
    b3  = 4.6;  // width back part
    l3  = 24;   // length back part
    dm  = 7.1;  // diameter
    h   = 0.4;  // material thickness

    if (hand_style == "modern") { /* ... */ }

    if (hand_style == "deco") {
        color("Black")
        linear_extrude(height = h)
        import("sekunden.svg");
    }
}
}
```

The module *clock_movement* received an additional parameter *hand_style*, with which the type of the hands can be set. Inside the hand submodules we use if-statements to differentiate the different styles. The style "modern" refers to the hands that we manually modeled before. The style "deco", however, loads the hand shapes from .svg files and then converts them into a 3D geometry using *linear_extrude*. The *import* function

Figure 7.4: In certain cases, slightly edited photos can serve as the basis for geometries

behaves here like any other 2D basic shape and can be used in the same way, e.g. it can be transformed.

Using the SVG import for complicated 2D geometries is generally the best way to use such geometries in OpenSCAD. However, it is not without effort to create such geometries even in programs specialized for this task such as Inkscape. In our use case, such an effort is not necessarily justified, since we use the hands primarily for visualization and have no requirements other than sound overall dimensions. In such a case, we can trade working time for computing time and let OpenSCAD create the 2D geometries directly from photos (Figure 7.4) for us. Unfortunately, the computation and memory required are not to be underestimated and it may happen that the procedure described below is not practical on a computer that is too weak. Fortunately, OpenSCAD caches the result of its calculations so they don't have to be done each time a preview is run! Let's see how we can extract our hands from .png images:

```
module clock_movement( time = [12, 0, 0], hand_style = "modern") {
    /* ... */
    module hour_hand() {
        /* ... */
        if (hand_style == "modern") { /* ... */ }
        if (hand_style == "deco")   { /* ... */ }

        if (hand_style == "classic") {
            lc = 61;

            color("Black")
            png_hands( "stunden.png", lc, h, [-9.5, -6.75, 0]);
        }
    }
```

```
module minute_hand() {
    /* ... */
    if (hand_style == "modern") { /* ... */ }
    if (hand_style == "deco")   { /* ... */ }

    if (hand_style == "classic") {
        lc = 84;

        color("Black")
        png_hands("minuten.png", lc, h, [-9, -6.75, 0]);
    }
}

module second_hand() {
    /* ... */
    if (hand_style == "modern") { /* ... */ }
    if (hand_style == "deco")   { /* ... */ }

    if (hand_style == "classic") {
        lc = 123;

        color("Black")
        png_hands("sekunden.png", lc, h, [-4,-36.8,0] );
    }
}

module png_hands(filename, length, height, displacement) {
    translate( displacement )
    linear_extrude( height = height )
    resize( [0, length], auto = true )
    projection( cut = true )
    translate( [0, 0, 75] )
    surface( filename, invert=true );
}
}
```

The new submodule *png_hands* creates a hand from a .png image file. First we use the *surface* geometry to create a height relief from a .png image file. Normally, light colors are interpreted as "high" and dark colors as "low". The parameter *invert* reverses this interpretation. We now move the resulting height relief upwards in such a way that it intersects the X-Y plane at a suitable point (Figure 7.5 on the left). If we now apply the *projection* transformation to the height relief, we intersect the relief in the X-Y plane and create a sufficiently clean 2D geometry from the intersection (Figure 7.5 right).

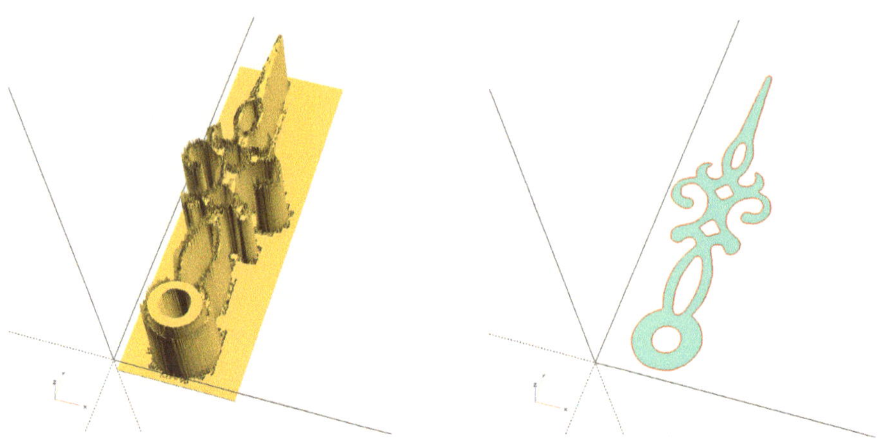

Figure 7.5: Using a *surface* geometry, 3D structures can be created from images (left), which can then be transformed into sufficiently clean 2D geometries using the *projection* transform (right)

Unfortunately, the resulting 2D geometry does not have the correct size. Therefore we use the *resize* transformation to scale the geometry to a desired length. We let the width to be determined automatically by setting it to 0. Afterwards we can extrude the now correctly scaled 2D geometry to the desired height and move it in such a way that the axis of the hand lies at the origin of the coordinate system.

To avoid spending this much compute every time you use the clock_movement module, it may be worthwhile to perform the calculation once and, after the *resize* operation, save the resulting 2D shape with OpenSCAD as an `.svg` file and then load it using *import* as described above.

7.3   Clean Library Interfaces

In principle, our clock movement module is now ready and could be included and used in other geometry descriptions using *use*. However, there is a flaw in our current approach. If you want to use the module in another geometry description, then you almost inevitably need information about the dimensions of the movement. However, these are not available to the other geometry description. An ad-hoc solution would be to open the movement module file and find out the values manually. A slightly less inelegant solution would be to define the variables defined inside the *clock_movement* module outside of the module. If you then include the `.scad` file using *include* instead of *use*, you can access these variables. However, there are two major problems with this solution. First, there can be name collisions. For example, we have defined the variables *width*, *depth* and *height* for the movement. There is a good chance that you would like to use these names in another project as well. It becomes even more difficult if you want to keep several modules in a library file, which all need their own variables. You can solve this problem with a strict naming convention. However, this is not a nice solution. The second big problem is that you have no control over which variables or information are "exported". The choice between *include* and *use* is a choice between "everything" or "nothing". If you choose "everything", then you lose the ability to define "local" variables outside of modules that are only available within the library. A better solution to this problem may be as follows:

```
// clock_movement constants
movement_data = [
    ["width",  56], // width of the main body
    ["depth",  56], // depth of the main body
    ["height", 20], // height of the main body

    ["alignment_dm",        14], // alignment diameter
    ["alignment_h",          1], // alignment height
    ["alignment_flat",       1], // alignment flattening
    ["alignment_notch_dm",   6], // alignment notch diameter
    ["alignment_notch_fl",   2], // alignment notch flattening

    ["screw_terminal_dm", 7.8], // screw terminal diameter
    ["screw_terminal_h",   5 ], // screw terminal height
                                // measured from main body

    ["hour_axle_dm", 5.1], // hour axle diameter
    ["hour_axle_h",  8.3], // hour axle height

    ["minute_axle_dm",  3.2], // minute axle diameter
    ["minute_axle_h",  12.1], // minute axle height

    ["second_axle_dm",  1  ], // second axle diameter
    ["second_axle_h",  14.5]  // second axle height
];

function movement_dim( name ) =
    [ for (d = movement_data) if (d[0] == name) d[1] ][0];
```

We create an array with data that we want to make available for our geometry. In our case, all important dimensions of our clock movement are in the array *movement_data*. To be able to access this data even if the library was included with *use*, we have to provide a function (here: *movement_dim*) for access. This function gets as parameter the name of the data entry whose data we want to read. One way to implement such a function is to use a generative for-loop. We scan with the loop variable *d* through the array *movement_data* and add an element (d[1]) to our result array if the passed *name* corresponds to the name of the array entry (if (d[0] == name)). The result of this generative for-loop is an array that contains only one entry: exactly the data we would like to read out of *movement_data*. What remains now is to access this one entry of the array. This is done by the subsequent [0] statement.

For more complicated searches over data OpenSCAD provides the *search* command. We can see how this can be used in the following example:

```
// hand_style constants
hands_data = [
    ["style",      "modern", "classic", "deco"],

    ["hour_l",      72.35,        61,    62.9],
    ["hour_r",       67.6,      56.6,   58.65],
    ["hour_w",          5,       1.5,       2],
    ["hour_h",        0.4,       0.4,     0.4],

    ["minute_l",    100.5,        84,   101.5],
    ["minute_r",       96,      79.5,   74.62],
    ["minute_w",        4,         1,       1],
    ["minute_h",      0.4,       0.4,     0.4],

    ["second_l",      134,       123,     120],
    ["second_r",       95,      88.4,   85.66],
    ["second_w",     1.25,       0.6,     0.7],
    ["second_h",      0.4,       0.4,     0.4]
];

function hands_dim( name, style ) =
    let (
        row = search( [name],  hands_data)[0],
        col = search( [style], hands_data[0])[0]
    ) hands_data[row][col];
```

We have summarized all data of the different hand types in one array. The access function *hands_ dim* has two parameters now. One for the name of the value and one for the name of the style. We use the expression *let* to find the indices of the row and column in which the requested data is located by using the search command. As before, a trailing `[0]` appears in our description, as the result returned by *search* is an array of indices and we are only interested in the first element of the array here. The first parameter to *search* is a list or array of search terms. Since we only want to search for one string at a time (*name* or *style*), the first parameter is written as an array with only one entry. The second parameter is the array to be searched. When searching for the matching row, we want to search through the complete field *hands_ data*. In this case *search* looks by default only at the first entry of the individual array entries, which are the names of the records. To find the matching column, we only search through the first entry of *hands_ data*, which is also an array. This way we get two indices *row* and *column*, with which we can then read the data we are looking for from the field *hands_ data* and return it as the function's value (`hands_data[row][column]`).

Of course it makes sense to use the functions *movement_ dim* and *hands_ dim* also within the module *clock_ movement* for the initialization of the variables:

```
module clock_movement( time = [12, 0, 0], hand_style = "modern") {

    width  = clockwork_dim("width");
    depth  = clockwork_dim("depth");
    height = clockwork_dim("height");

    alignment_dm        = clockwork_dim("alignment_dm");
    alignment_h         = clockwork_dim("alignment_h");
    alignment_flat      = clockwork_dim("alignment_flat");
    alignment_notch_dm  = clockwork_dim("alignment_notch_dm");
    alignment_notch_fl  = clockwork_dim("alignment_notch_fl");

    screw_terminal_dm = clockwork_dim("screw_terminal_dm");
    screw_terminal_h  = clockwork_dim("screw_terminal_h");

    hour_axle_dm = clockwork_dim("hour_axle_dm");
    hour_axle_h  = clockwork_dim("hour_axle_h");

    minute_axle_dm = clockwork_dim("minute_axle_dm");
    minute_axle_h  = clockwork_dim("minute_axle_h");
```

```
    second_axle_dm = clockwork_dim("second_axle_dm");
    second_axle_h  = clockwork_dim("second_axle_h");

    /* ... */

    module hour_hand() {

        h = hands_dim("hour_h",hand_style);
        l = hands_dim("hour_l",hand_style);
        r = hands_dim("hour_r",hand_style);
        b = hands_dim("hour_w",hand_style);

        /* ... */
    }

    module minute_hand() {

        h = hands_dim("minute_h",hand_style);
        l = hands_dim("minute_l",hand_style);
        r = hands_dim("minute_r",hand_style);
        b = hands_dim("minute_w",hand_style);

        /* ... */
    }

    module second_hand() {

        h = hands_dim("second_h",hand_style);
        l = hands_dim("second_l",hand_style);
        r = hands_dim("second_r",hand_style);
        b = hands_dim("second_w",hand_style);

        /* ... */
    }

    /* ... */

}
```

7.4   Animate the Movement

OpenSCAD offers a simple way to animate our geometries and, if chosen, save the animation as an image sequence. To animate our clockwork, we can extend our geometry description outside the module *clock_movement* as follows:

```
/* ... */

function get_time( tick ) = [(tick / 3600) % 12, (tick / 60) % 60, tick % 60];

clock_movement( get_time($t * 43200) , "modern");
```

We define a function *get_time* to which we can give a number of seconds as a parameter and get a three-dimensional vector with hours, minutes and seconds as a result. The % operator stands for the modulo or remainder of a division and ensures that the minute and second values always lie in the range 0 to 59 and that the hour value always lies in the range 0 to 11. We now pass the expression '$t * 43200' as a parameter to the *get_time* function. The special variable *$t* returns the current time within an animation. The animation time is always a floating point number that runs between 0 and 1. Thus, we scale the animation time with the expression to the range 0 to 43200 (12 hours have 43200 seconds).

To start the animation, you have to make the animation menu visible (*View -> Animate*). Three input fields *Time*, *FPS* and *Steps* will then appear under the output window. As *Steps* we enter 43200 and as *FPS* a 1. Our clock should start moving and ticking away. You can stop the animation by hiding the animation menu (*View -> Animate*). If you check the *Dump Pictures* checkbox, every animation step will be saved as a numbered .png file. These files can then be used afterwards, e.g., to convert them into a video file. Under Linux this can be done with the program *ffmpeg*.

Project 5: Pen Holder

In this project, we want to construct a pen holder that has plenty of space for our desk utensils and can be 3D printed without support structure. The design will be inspired by Gothic architecture.

8.1   What's new?

We learn about the rotate extrusion transform. In addition, we use an exploratory design approach this time that develops the final module "from the inside out".

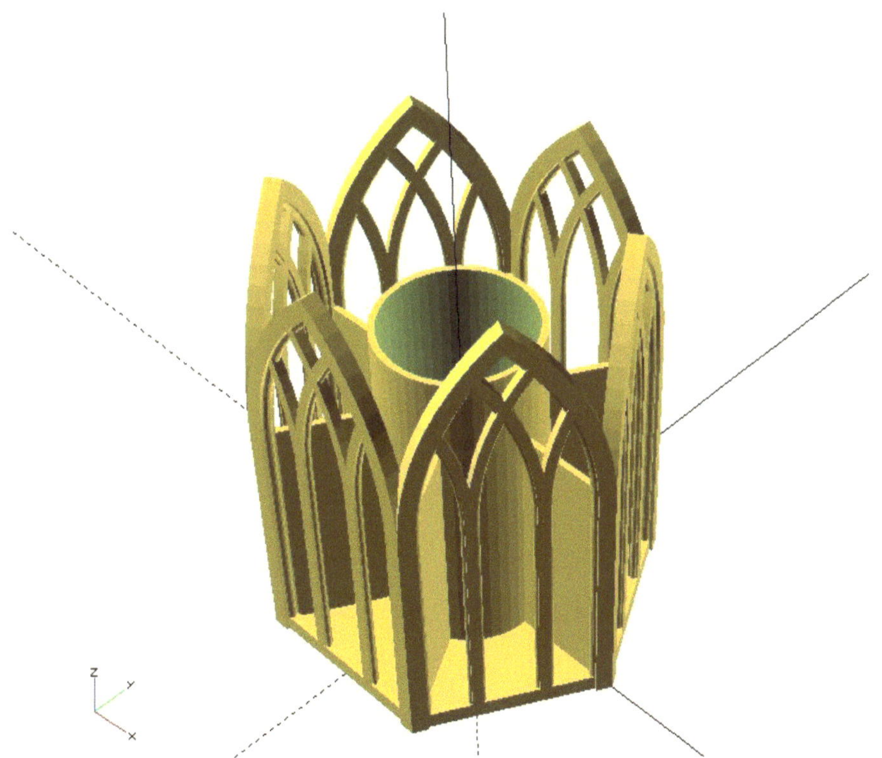

Figure 8.1: Pencil holder with Gothic style elements

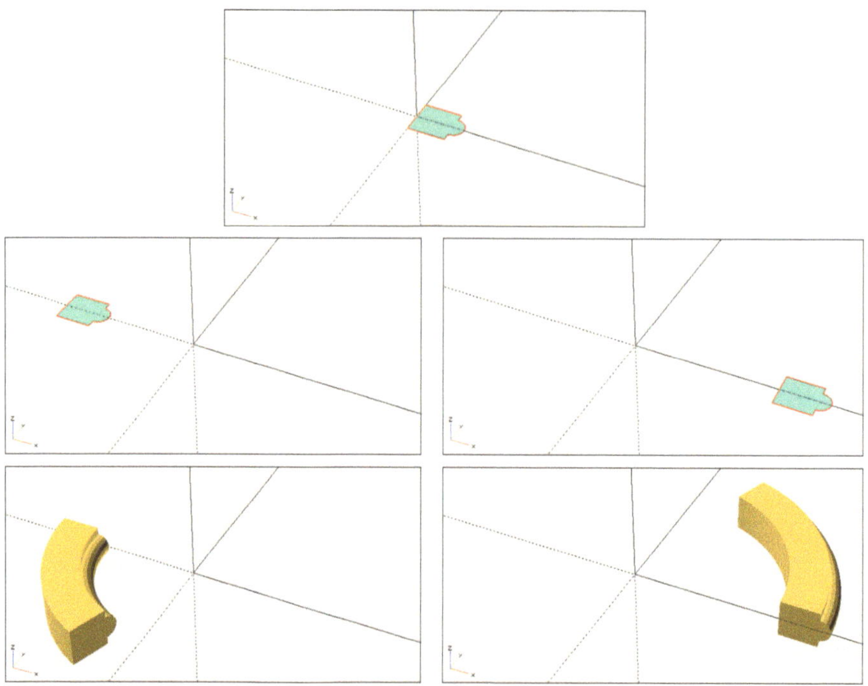

Figure 8.2: The result of the rotate_extrude transform depends on where the underlying 2D geometry was originally positioned along the X-axis.

8.2   Let's go

Core element of the pen holder are Gothic-looking arches on the outside. To create these arches, the rotate extrusion transform is a good choice. Similar to the linear extrusion, *rotate_extrude* acts on a 2D geometry and creates a 3D object from it. Unlike *linear_extrude*, however, the 2D geometry is not extruded along a straight line but along an (implicit) curve.

The *rotate_extrude* transformation takes some time to get used to as some of its properties are implicitly given by the position of the 2D geometry that is being extruded. Approximately, *rotate_extrude* operates the following way: first, the given 2D geometry is set upright by rotating it around the X-axis. Then the geometry is extruded by rotating it clockwise around the Z-axis. Thus, the resulting 3D geometry depends a lot on where the 2D geometry was located initially (Figure 8.2).

Let's start our arch with a 2D geometry consisting of a square and a circle:

```
arch_base   = 5;
arch_angle  = 70;
arch_radius = 20;

rotate( [-90, 0, 0])
rotate_extrude( angle = arch_angle, $fn = 100 )
translate( [-arch_radius, 0] )
union(){
    translate( [0, -arch_base / 2] )
    square( arch_base );

    translate( [arch_base, 0] )
    circle( d = arch_base * 3 / 5, $fn = 18);
}
```

We create a square with side length *arch_base* and move it to the center of the X-axis. Since we are in two dimensions, our translate transformation requires only a two-dimensional vector as input. Additionally, we define a circle, which has a diameter of 3/5 of the square size and position the circle at the outer edge of the square. We connect the square and the circle to a joint 2D geometry using a Boolean union.

Now we can set the radius of our arch by moving the 2D geometry along the X axis away from the origin. Since we want the circle of our geometry to be on the inside of the arch, we move our geometry in the negative X-direction (**translate([-arch_radius, 0])**). Only after this translation we can apply the *rotate_extrude* transform to create our arch piece. The parameter *angle* specifies how far the 2D geometry should be rotationally extruded. An angle of 360 degrees would result in a closed ring. In older versions of OpenSCAD, no angle could be specified and a closed ring was always generated. After the rotational extrusion, the arch piece lies on its side. With a rotation around the X-axis we can finally set the arc upright.

To create the opposite side of the arch, we can simply use a combination of for-loop and mirror transformation:

```
arch_base   = 5;
arch_angle  = 70;
arch_radius = 20;

```

```
for (m = [0:1])
mirror( [m, 0, 0] )
rotate( [-90, 0, 0])
rotate_extrude( angle = arch_angle, $fn = 100 )
translate( [-arch_radius, 0] )
union(){
    translate( [0, -arch_base / 2] )
    square( arch_base );

    translate( [arch_base, 0] )
    circle( d = arch_base * 3 / 5, $fn = 18);
}
```

The loop variable *m* takes the value 0 and the value 1 exactly once and thus creates a normal and a mirrored version of our arch piece. However, there is now a gap between our arches that we still need to close. The problem is that our original arch piece does not directly touch the Z axis with its top edge at the end of the arch. This creates a gap when we mirror it. So we have to move our arch piece to touch the Z-axis before mirroring:

```
arch_base   = 5;
arch_angle  = 70;
arch_radius = 20;

for (m = [0:1])
mirror( [m, 0, 0] )
translate( [cos(arch_angle) * arch_radius, 0, 0] )
rotate( [-90, 0, 0])
rotate_extrude( angle = arch_angle, $fn = 100 )
translate( [-arch_radius, 0] )
union(){
    translate( [0, -arch_base / 2] )
    square( arch_base );

    translate( [arch_base, 0] )
    circle( d = arch_base * 3 / 5, $fn = 18);
}
```

It turns out that the distance to the Z-axis can be described by cos(arch_angle) * arch_radius. This is not obvious at first. It helps to sketch the situation on a piece of paper to identify the "suitable" right triangle and then use the cosine… (*cos(α) = adjacent / hypotenuse*).

If we now play a little with the parameters *arch_radius* and *arch_angle*, we see that the two halves of the arc always meet neatly. For further use of our arch, the previous parameterization is a bit uncomfortable. Ideally, we would prefer to specify the width of the complete arch from outer edge to outer edge and calculate the radius to match. This can be done in the following way:

```
arch_width  = 50;
arch_base   = 5;
arch_angle  = 70;
arch_radius = arch_width / (2 - 2 * cos(arch_angle) );


for (m = [0:1])
mirror( [m, 0, 0] )
translate( [cos(arch_angle) * arch_radius, 0, 0] )
rotate( [-90, 0, 0])
rotate_extrude( angle = arch_angle, $fn = 100 )
translate( [-arch_radius, 0] )
union(){
    translate( [0, -arch_base / 2] )
    square( arch_base );

    translate( [arch_base, 0] )
    circle( d = arch_base * 3 / 5, $fn = 18);
}
```

In this case, too, it is helpful to sketch out the whole thing and set up an equation that establishes a relationship between *arch_angle*, *arch_radius* and *arch_width*. You can then transform this equation so that *arch_radius* is singled out on one side of the equal sign.

The last thing missing are two vertical columns below our arch. We can describe them with the same basic shape and a linear extrusion. Lastly, we can now package the whole thing into a module:

```
module arch(
    arch_width,
    arch_base,
    arch_angle,
    pillar_height
) {

    arch_radius = arch_width / (2 - 2 * cos(arch_angle) );
```

```openscad
module basic_shape() {
    union(){
        translate( [0, -arch_base / 2] )
        square( arch_base );

        translate( [arch_base, 0] )
        circle( d = arch_base * 3 / 5, $fn = 18);
    }
}

translate( [0, 0, pillar_height] )
for (m = [0:1])
mirror( [m, 0, 0] )
translate( [cos(arch_angle) * arch_radius, 0, 0] )
union(){
    rotate( [-90, 0, 0])
    rotate_extrude( angle = arch_angle, $fn = 100 )
    translate( [-arch_radius, 0] )
    basic_shape();

    translate( [0, 0, -pillar_height] )
    linear_extrude( height = pillar_height )
    translate( [-arch_radius, 0] )
    basic_shape();
    }
}

arch(
    arch_width    = 50,
    arch_base     = 5,
    arch_angle    = 75,
    pillar_height = 50
);
```

We have made the variables *arch_width*, *arch_base* and *arch_angle* parameters of the new module *arch* and added a new parameter *pillar_height*. Inside the module we encapsulated our 2D base shape into a submodule because we need the base shape in two places - for the arch and for the pillars. At the point where we set our original arch piece upright by rotating it around the X-axis, we split the geometry description of the arch and inserted a Boolean union. This way, we can add a pillar below the arch, that will then be shifted and mirrored in tandem with the arch.

There is still one flaw in our geometry description. If we use small angles, e.g. 30 degrees, then the tips of the mirrored arch parts "break through" each other. To prevent this, we need to trim the tips. We can do this with a Boolean difference operation, which we place just before the mirror transform:

```
/* ... */

    translate( [0, 0, pillar_height] )
    for (m = [0:1])
    mirror( [m, 0, 0] )
    difference(){
        translate( [cos(arch_angle) * arch_radius, 0, 0] )
        union(){
            rotate( [-90, 0, 0])
            rotate_extrude( angle = arch_angle, $fn = 100 )
            translate( [-arch_radius, 0] )
            basic_shape();

            translate( [0, 0, -pillar_height] )
            linear_extrude( height = pillar_height )
            translate( [-arch_radius, 0] )
            basic_shape();
        }

        translate([
            0,
            -arch_base,
            sin(arch_angle) * arch_radius - 5 * arch_base
        ])
        cube( 5 * arch_base);
    }

/* ... */
```

Now we can use our module *arch* to define one side of our pen holder. To do this, we instantiate the module several times with adjusted parameters in each case and position the individual parts relative to each other in a suitable way:

```
arch_width    = 60;
arch_base     = 5;
arch_angle    = 50;
pillar_height = 75;
```

```
// main arch
arch(
    arch_width,
    arch_base,
    arch_angle,
    pillar_height
);

width_factor = 2 / 3;
base_factor  = 3 / 5;

// inner arches
displacement_x1 =
    (arch_width -
     arch_width * width_factor -
     arch_base / 2) / 2;

for(v = [-1:2:1])
translate( [displacement_x1*v, 0, 0] )
arch(
    arch_width * width_factor,
    arch_base * base_factor,
    arch_angle * 0.82,
    pillar_height
);

// inner side arches
displacement_x2 =
    (arch_width -
     arch_width * (1 - width_factor) -
     arch_base / 2) / 2;

for(v = [-1:2:1])
translate( [displacement_x2*v, 0, 0] )
arch(
    arch_width * (1 - width_factor),
    arch_base * base_factor,
    arch_angle * 0.58,
    pillar_height
);
```

The resulting geometry description is not very complicated, but a bit confusing. If you are confronted with such a description and want to get an overview of which part of the geometry description corresponds to which component in the output window, the highlighting of individual parts by means of a preceding # character is very helpful. As with the description of a single arch, we use for-loops to create local copies of the geometry where needed. In this case, the subsequent geometry description is not mirrored, but translated once in the negative and once in the positive direction along the X-axis. This is achieved by the loop variable taking on the values -1 and 1. To prevent the loop variable from becoming 0 on its way from -1 to 1 we set the step size to 2.

Now we can encapsulate our single side into a module and let the module *arch* become a submodule of this new module:

```
module side_piece(
    arch_width,
    arch_base,
    arch_angle,
    pillar_height
) {

    module arch(
        arch_width,
        arch_base,
        arch_angle,
        pillar_height
    ) {
        /* ... */
    }

    // main arch
    // inner arches
    // inner side arches

    /* ... */
}

arch_width    = 60;
arch_base     = 5;
arch_angle    = 50;
pillar_height = 75;

side_piece(
    arch_width,
    arch_base,
    arch_angle,
    pillar_height
);
```

Although the module *side_piece* and its submodule *arch* now have parameters with the same name, there is no confusion (at least not on the side of OpenSCAD). The respective "inner" variables cover the "outer" ones. So in the module *arch* the parameter *arch_width* of the module *side_piece* is no longer visible. Only the parameter *arch_width* of the module *arch* can be accessed.

Now we can use the *side_piece* module to describe our pen holder. Let's start with a hexagonal arrangement:

```
arch_width    = 60;
arch_base     = 5;
arch_angle    = 50;
pillar_height = 75;

hexagonal_height = arch_width / ( 2 * tan(30) );

for (r = [0:60:359])
rotate( [0, 0, r] )
translate( [0, hexagonal_height - arch_base / 2, 0] )
side_piece(
    arch_width,
    arch_base,
    arch_angle,
    pillar_height
);
```

To create a hexagon, we need to move the side piece a specific distance along the Y-axis and then rotate (and copy) it 5 times by 60 degrees around the Z-axis. To determine this specific distance we have to calculate the distance of the hexagon sides to the center of the hexagon. Again, it helps to sketch out the elements in question on a piece of paper. The perpendicular line from the center of the hexagon to the center of a hexagon side has an angle of 30 degrees to the radius of the hexagon. The radius is the hypotenuse in the resulting triangle. The central, perpendicular line is the adjacent and half of the hexagon side is the opposite. As the tangent of an angle is equal to the adjacent divided by the opposite (and we are interested in the adjacent), `opposite / tan(30)` gives us the length we are looking for. Since the opposite is half of the hexagon side that has length *arch_width*, we finally end up with the formula `(arch_width / 2) / tan(30)`, which in turn can also be written as `arch_width / (2 * tan(30) )`.

Since we have constructed the side pieces centered on the X-axis, we need to translate them by `arch_base / 2` less than just calculated. Next we describe the base of the pen holder and its border:

```
arch_width    = 60;
arch_base     = 5;
arch_angle    = 50;
pillar_height = 75;

bottom_thickness = 1;
border_height    = 5;
border_thickness = 3;

hexagonal_height = arch_width / ( 2 * tan(30) );

for (r = [0:60:359])
rotate( [0, 0, r] )
translate( [0, hexagonal_height - arch_base / 2, 0] )
union() {
    side_piece(
        arch_width,
        arch_base,
        arch_angle,
        pillar_height
    );

    // bottom plate
    translate( [-arch_width / 2, -hexagonal_height, 0] )
    cube( [arch_width, hexagonal_height, bottom_thickness] );

    // border
    translate( [-arch_width / 2, -border_thickness / 2, 0] )
    cube( [arch_width, border_thickness, border_height] );
}
```

We simply take advantage of the symmetry of the hexagon and describe only one part of the bottom panel and one part of the border at a time, and then use a Boolean union to align and rotate these parts together with the side piece.

Finally, we take care of the inner geometry of the pen holder. It consists of a hollow cylinder and six inner walls:

```
/* ... */

cylinder_dm     = 50;
cylinder_height = 100;
cylinder_walls  = 2;

hexagonal_height = arch_width / ( 2 * tan(30) );
hexagonal_radius = arch_width / ( 2 * sin(30) );

/* ... */

// center cylinder
difference() {
    cylinder( d = cylinder_dm, h = cylinder_height ,$fn = 50);

    translate( [0, 0, bottom_thickness] )
    cylinder(
        d = cylinder_dm - 2 * cylinder_walls,
        h = cylinder_height ,
        $fn = 50
    );
}

// inner walls
for (r = [0:60:359])
rotate( [0, 0, r] )
translate( [cylinder_dm/2 - 0.1, -cylinder_walls / 2, 0] )
cube([
    hexagonal_radius - cylinder_dm/2 - arch_base / 2,
    cylinder_walls,
    pillar_height
]);
```

We create the hollow cylinder in the center by means of a Boolean difference operation, where we subtract a second, smaller and upward shifted cylinder. For the inner walls we now need the radius of the hexagon. You can derive the radius using the same reasoning as before. Only that one does not use the tangent here but the sine. The inner walls consist of a rectangle, which is first shifted appropriately and then rotated (and copied) five times by 60 degrees.

8.3   3D printing tips

The overhangs in our pen holder are kept small enough such that you should be able to print the holder without a support structure. Printing becomes more challenging the larger we choose *arch_angle*. If you have problems printing the overhangs, try reducing the layer height in your slicer program. Alternatively or additionally, you can try to increase the line width. With a typical 0.4 millimeter nozzle you should be able to print line widths of 0.5 to 0.6 millimeters without any problems. Last but not least, you can also try to reduce the printing speed. In that case the blower at the print nozzle has more time to cool down the freshly printed plastic.

Project 6: Stamp

In this project we will model a stamp whose geometry automatically adjusts to the size of the text with which the stamp is parameterized.

9.1   What's new?

We will work with the 2D basic shape *text* and see that a certain limitation of OpenSCAD makes our life particularly hard when using *text*. We will work around this limitation in a tricky way and the Boolean operation *intersection* as well as the *projection* transform will help us with that. Furthermore we will get to know the *offset*, *minkowski* and *scale* transformations and test out how to operate OpenSCAD from the command line.

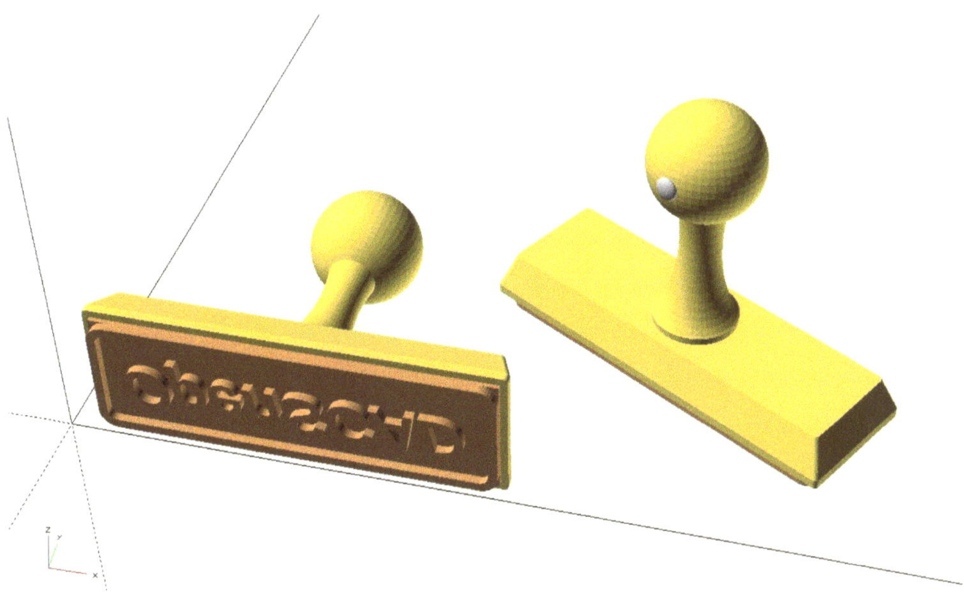

Figure 9.1: A parameterizable stamp

9.2   Let's go

Let's start by defining a basic structure for our model description. We define a module *stamp* and two submodules *relief* and *stamp_body*. We split the stamp geometry into two submodules as we may want to 3D print the stamp relief and the stamp body separately, e.g. to be able to use different printing materials:

```openscad
module stamp (
    txt,                        // stamp text
    font_size,                  // approx. height of letter
    font          = "Liberation Sans:style=Bold Italic",
    stamp_depth   = 2,          // depth of the stamp relief
){

    module relief() {
        // text
        linear_extrude( height = stamp_depth )
        text(
            text = txt,
            size = font_size,
            font = font,
            valign = "center",
            halign = "center",
            $fn = 50
        );
    }

    module stamp_body() {

    }

    color("Peru")
    relief();

    stamp_body();

}

stamp("OpenSCAD",10);
```

Our module *stamp* has four parameters for now. The parameter *txt* sets the text of the stamp, the parameter *font_size* sets the (maximum) height of a regular capital letter in millimeters and the parameter *font* sets the font to be used. An overview of the fonts available in OpenSCAD can be found in the menu under *Help -> Font List*. The fourth parameter *stamp_depth* defines the depth of the stamp relief.

In the *relief* submodule we use the 2D base shape *text* to generate a two-dimensional geometry of the stamp text. We set the vertical and horizontal alignment of the font (*valign* and *halign*) to *center* and pass *txt*, *font size* and *font type* as further parameters. As with circles, spheres or cylinders, we can specify the level of detail of the geometry with the special variable *$fn*. We can use the resulting text geometry like any other 2D basic shape. In this case we extrude (*linear_extrude*) the text to the desired depth of the stamp relief.

To continue in our model description, it would be useful if we could get the width and height of the text. The height will be similar to the font size. The width depends on the particular *txt*. It may be surprising, but there is no way in OpenSCAD to find out these dimensions! This limitation of OpenSCAD makes it very difficult to define geometries that automatically adapt to a given text. We're going to try it anyway, and we have to dig deep into our bag of tricks to do it. We start by defining another submodule *text_area* and create the text inside of it again as a 2D base shape and extrude it to 3 millimeters:

```
module stamp (
    /* ... */
){

    module text_area() {
        linear_extrude( height = 3)
        text(
            text = txt,
            size = font_size,
            font = font,
            valign = "center",
            halign = "center",
            $fn = 50
        );
    }

    !text_area(); // debug

    /* ... */
}
```

It is advisable to instantiate the *text_area* submodule once under the module definition and prefix the instance with a ! character. This way you can better follow the step-by-step construction of the *text_area* module. Now things get tricky. We set our text upright by rotating it 90 degrees around the X-axis. Then we use the *projection* transform to project the standing text onto the X-Y plane and connect the projected "shadows" of each letter using the *hull* transformation:

```
module stamp (
    /* ... */
){

    module text_area() {
        hull()
        projection()
        rotate([90,0,0])
        linear_extrude( height = 3)
        text(
            text = txt,
            size = font_size,
            font = font,
            valign = "center",
            halign = "center",
            $fn = 50
        );
    }

    !text_area(); // debug

    /* ... */
}
```

It is a good idea to follow the described steps individually by means of preview (*F5*) or render (*F6*) (Figure 9.2). If you use render instead of preview, the 2D shapes will be better recognizable as such.

We have made some progress in determining the text area. We now have a 2D shape that has the width of our text. Let's just apply the trick again, only now we don't rotate around the X-axis, but around the Y-axis:

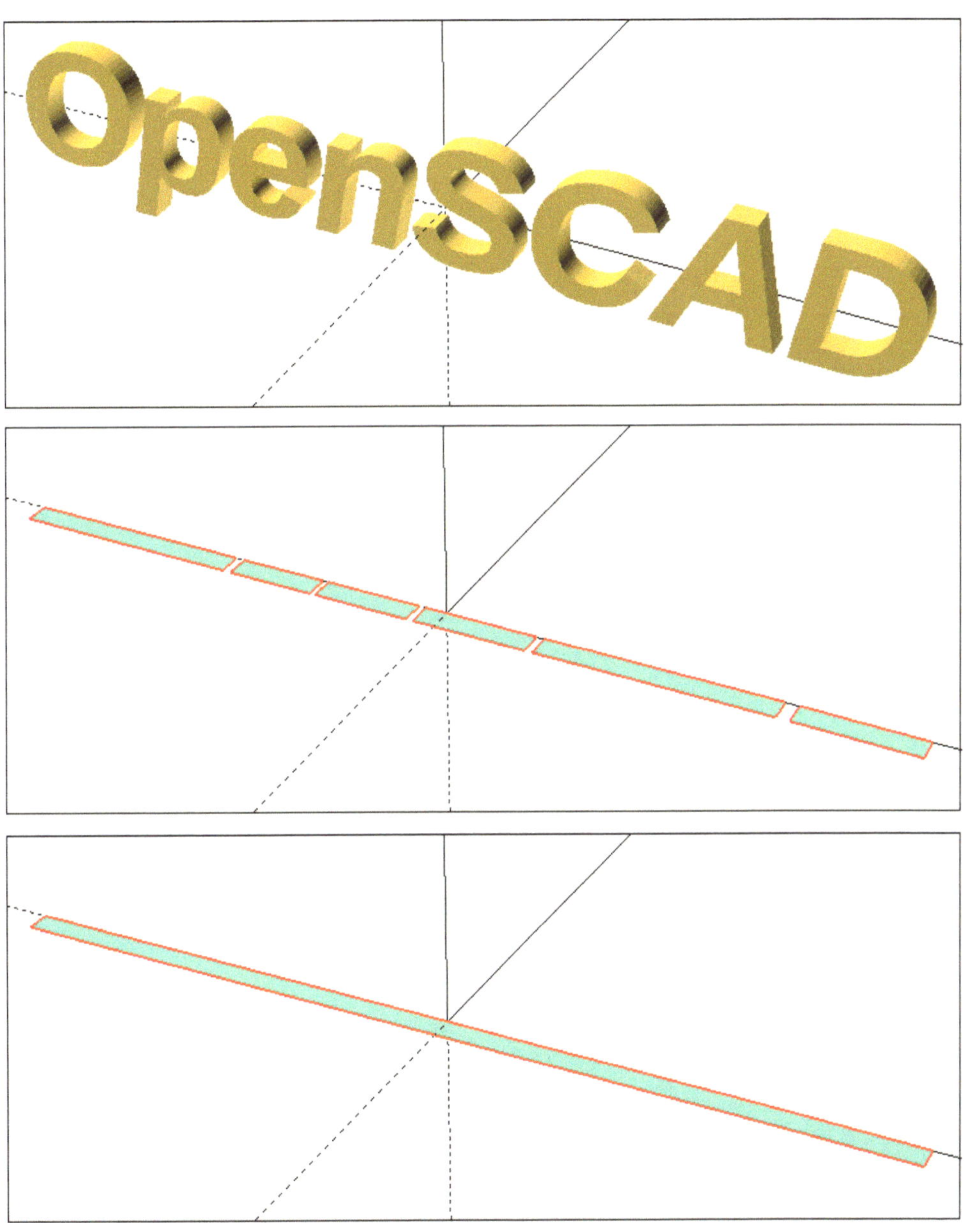

Figure 9.2: By using *projection* and *hull* we get a rectangle that has the width of the text

```
module stamp( /* ... */ ) {

    module text_area() {
        hull()
        projection()
        rotate([90,0,0])
        linear_extrude( height = 3)
        text(
            text = txt,
            size = font_size,
            font = font,
            valign = "center",
            halign = "center",
            $fn = 50
        );

        hull()
        projection()
        rotate( [0, 90, 0] )
        linear_extrude( height = 1 )
        text(
            text = txt,
            size = font_size,
            font = font,
            valign = "center",
            halign = "center",
            $fn = 50
        );
    }
    /* ... */
}
```

Now we have another 2D shape representing the height of our text. Note that this time
we have only extruded by one millimeter. What we're missing now is a way to combine
these two 2D shapes. If we extrude each of the shapes by a suitable length and then
superimpose them, the intersection of these two shapes should have exactly the geometry
we are looking for. For the "suitable length" of the first shape, we need to estimate what
the maximum height of the text will be. Here we can simply assume '3 x font size'. For
the length we can take the number of characters in the text, multiply this by the font
size and then use a safety factor of two. With these values we can now extrude the 2D
shapes and let them overlap using rotate and translate transforms:

```openscad
module stamp( /* ... */ ) {

    module text_area() {
        estimated_length = len(txt) * font_size * 2;

        translate( [0,0,-1] )
        rotate([-90,0,0])
        translate([0,0,-(3 * font_size) / 2])
        linear_extrude( height = 3 * font_size )
        hull()
        projection()
        rotate([90,0,0])
        linear_extrude( height = 3)
        text(
            text = txt,
            size = font_size,
            font = font,
            valign = "center",
            halign = "center",
            $fn = 50
        );

        rotate( [0, -90, 0] )
        translate( [0, 0, -estimated_length/2] )
        linear_extrude( height = estimated_length )
        hull()
        projection()
        rotate( [0, 90, 0] )
        linear_extrude( height = 1 )
        text(
            text = txt,
            size = font_size,
            font = font,
            valign = "center",
            halign = "center",
            $fn = 50
        );
    }
    /* ... */
}
```

Note the use of the *len* function to get the number of characters of the stamp text. In the same way, the *len* function also allows to get the number of elements in an array. We are almost there! We can now use the Boolean operation *intersection* to create the intersection of our two 3D shapes and then apply another *projection* transform to convert it back to a 2D shape:

```
module stamp( /* ... */ ) {
    module text_area() {
        estimated_length = len(txt) * font_size * 2;

        projection()
        intersection(){
            translate( [0,0,-1] )
            rotate([-90,0,0])
            translate([0,0,-(3 * font_size) / 2])
            linear_extrude( height = 3 * font_size )
            hull()
            projection()
            rotate([90,0,0])
            linear_extrude( height = 3)
            text(
                text = txt,
                size = font_size,
                font = font,
                valign = "center",
                halign = "center",
                $fn = 50
            );

            rotate( [0, -90, 0] )
            translate( [0, 0, -estimated_length/2] )
            linear_extrude( height = estimated_length )
            hull()
            projection()
            rotate( [0, 90, 0] )
            linear_extrude( height = 1 )
            text(
                text = txt,
                size = font_size,
                font = font,
                valign = "center",
                halign = "center",
                $fn = 50
            );
        }
    }
    /* ... */
}
```

Figure 9.3: Done! A 2D surface that automatically adapts to the dimension of the text

If you now remove the ! character again and run a preview (*F5*) you can see that we have reached our goal (Figure 9.3). We have created a 2D surface that can automatically adjust to the size of the stamp text! We will now use this special surface to construct the rest of the stamp. Before we continue, we should make sure that we remove our "debug" instance of the *text_area* now.

Let us return to the *relief* submodule and use our *text_area* module to describe the relief background:

```
module stamp (
    txt,                        // stamp text
    font_size,                  // approx. height of letter
    font          = "Liberation Sans:style=Bold Italic",
    stamp_depth  = 2,           // depth of the stamp relief
    stamp_margin = 5,           // margin of the text

    stamp_relief_depth = 2,     // depth of the relief substrate
){
    /* ... */
    module relief() {
        // text
        linear_extrude( height = stamp_depth )
        text(
            text = txt,
            size = font_size,
            font = font,
            valign = "center",
            halign = "center",
```

```
                $fn = 50
        );

        // relief base
        translate( [0, 0, stamp_depth] )
        linear_extrude( height = stamp_relief_depth )
        offset( delta = stamp_margin )
        text_area();
    }
    /* ... */
}
```

We extend our module *stamp* with the parameters *stamp_margin* and *stamp_relief_depth*, which define the margin around the text and the depth of the relief background. We model the relief background based on the *text_area* and extend it with the transformation *offset*. This transformation expands the subsequent 2D geometry by the parameter *delta* or shrinks the geometry if *delta* is negative. Then we extrude our expanded *text_area* to *stamp_relief_depth* and position it above the stamp text using a translate transformation (`translate( [0, 0, stamp depth] )`).

It would be nice if we could optionally add a border to our stamp text. We can construct such a border based on our *text_area* as well:

```
module stamp (
    txt,                        // stamp text
    font_size,                  // approx. height of letter
    font          = "Liberation Sans:style=Bold Italic",
    stamp_depth  = 2,           // depth of the stamp relief
    stamp_margin = 5,           // margin of the text

    stamp_relief_depth = 2,     // depth of the relief substrate

    border            = true,   // enable text border
    border_thickness = 2,       // text border thickness
    border_radius    = 2,       // text border radius
){
    /* ... */
    module relief() {
        // text
        linear_extrude( height = stamp_depth )
        text(
            text = txt,
            size = font_size,
```

```
            font = font,
            valign = "center",
            halign = "center",
            $fn = 50
        );

        // relief base
        translate( [0, 0, stamp_depth] )
        linear_extrude( height = stamp_relief_depth)
        offset(delta = stamp_margin + (border ? border_thickness : 0))
        text_area();

        // border
        if (border) {

            linear_extrude( height = stamp_depth )
            difference(){
                minkowski(){
                    offset( delta = stamp_margin - border_radius )
                    text_area();

                    circle( r = border_radius + border_thickness, $fn = 36);
                }

                minkowski(){
                    offset(delta = stamp_margin - border_radius)
                    text_area();

                    circle( r = border_radius, $fn = 36);
                }
            }
        }
    }
    /* ... */
}
```

For the optional border we extend the module *stamp* with three more parameters (*border,
border_thickness* and *border_radius*) that characterize the border. First, we adjust our
relief background. If there is a border, then we add the width of the border to the *delta*
parameter of the offset transformation.

We model the border within an if-statement, such that the border only becomes part of
the geometry description if the *border* parameter is set to *true*. We construct the border
itself as a Boolean difference of two 2D geometries, which we subsequently convert to a
3D geometry using *linear_extrude*. The two 2D geometries are two Minkowski sums.

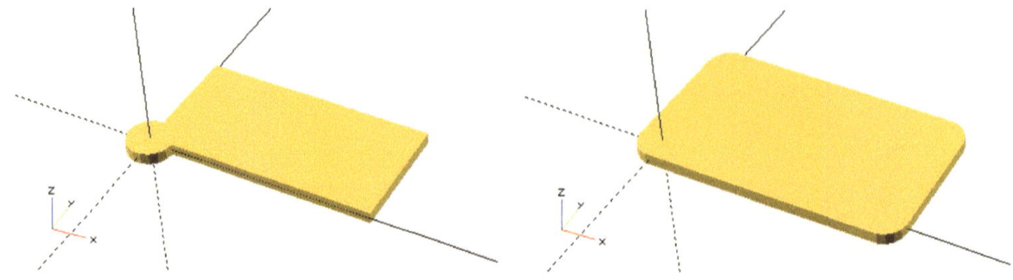

Figure 9.4: Minkowski sum (right) of a rectangle and a circle (left)

The Minkowski sum of two point sets is the set of the pairwise summed points from both sets. In the case of the Minkowski sum of a rectangle and a circle, we can simply imagine that the circle is copied to all four corners of the rectangle and then the convex hull of the whole is formed (Figure 9.4).

We use the *minkowski* transformation to give the *text_area*-based border rounded corners. We need two surfaces. A large one that describes the outer edge of the border and a small one that describes the inner edge of the border. The smaller area is then subtracted from the larger one. Since the *minkowski* transformation adds the radius of the circle to the overall dimension of the *text_area*, we must consider the radius within the earlier *offset* transformation and subtract it from the *border*.

Since the *minkowski* transformation can't deal with a situation where the radius of the circles becomes 0, we have to add another if-statement:

```
module stamp( /* ... */ ) {
    /* ... */
    module relief() {
        /* ... */
        // border
        if (border) {

            linear_extrude( height = stamp_depth )
            difference() {
                minkowski(){
                    offset(
                        delta = stamp_margin -
                                border_radius +
                                ((border_radius > 0) ? 0 : border_thickness)
                    )
                    text_area();
```

```
                    if (border_radius > 0)
                        circle( r = border_radius + border_thickness, $fn = 36);
                }

                minkowski(){
                    offset(delta = stamp_margin - border_radius)
                    text_area();

                    if (border_radius > 0)
                        circle( r = border_radius, $fn = 36);
                }
            }
        }
    }
    /* ... */
}
```

Now the circles within the Minkowski sums are only present in the geometry description if the radius of the circles is greater than 0. At the same time the *offset* transformation of the larger area is adapted in such a way that in case of a radius of zero the thickness of the border is not produced via the circle but via the *offset* transformation.

With this, we have completed the description of the stamp relief and can now turn to the geometry description of the stamp body:

```
module stamp (
    /* ... */
    stamp_relief   = true,      // generate stamp relief
    stamp_body     = true,      // generate stamp body

    body_height    = 10,        // stamp body height
    body_base      = 2,         // height of stamp body base
    body_border    = 1.6,       // wall thickness of relief mount
    body_allowance = 0.5,       // expansion of relief mount when printing in
                                // two parts
    body_inner_depth   = 1,     // depth of relief mount
    body_radius        = 1,     // stamp body edge radius
    body_taper         = 3,     // stamp body taper
    body_handle_dm     = 25,    // handle sphere diameter
    body_handle_height = 40,    // handle sphere height above body
    body_handle_collar = 3,     // lower handle collar
    body_handle_ind    = 5      // diameter of the front indicator
){
    /* ... */
```

```
    module stamp_body() {

        body_z_null = stamp_depth + stamp_relief_depth - body_inner_depth;

        module base( taper = 0) {
            minkowski() {
                offset(
                    delta = stamp_margin +
                            (border ? border_thickness : 0) +
                            body_border +
                            (stamp_relief ? 0 : body_allowance) -
                            body_radius -
                            taper
                )
                text_area();

                if (body_radius > 0)
                circle( r = body_radius, $fn = 36);
            }
        }
    }
    /* ... */
}
```

We begin by extending our module *stamp* by quite a number of parameters again. The parameters *stamp_relief* and *stamp_body* stand out in particular. They control whether a geometry description is generated for the relief or the stamp body. We will use this information not only when instantiating the submodules, but also within the submodule *stamp_body*. We refrain from a detailed description of the numerous other parameters at this point, since their meaning will become clear in the following sections.

In the submodule *stamp_body* we first define the variable *body_z_null*, which describes the height of the lower edge of the stamp body. Since the body will have a recess on the bottom side to accommodate the stamp relief, the bottom edge is not equal to `stamp_depth + stamp_relief_depth` but lower by `body_inner_depth`. Next, we define an auxiliary module *base* that provides a two-dimensional description of the stamp body's base shape. Like the stamp relief, this base shape builds on *text_area*, which is expanded using the *offset* transformation and rounded using the *minkowski* transformation. The expansion of the base area depends on a number of parameters and considers e.g. if there is a border or not. Via the parameter *taper* the base area can be adjusted in the further course of the model description without having to use another *offset* transformation.

The check whether a *stamp_relief* is created together with a *stamp_body* has the following background: if the stamp relief is not created together with the stamp body, we assume that the stamp body and stamp relief are printed separately and joined together afterwards. In this case, the parameter *body_allowance* allows to adjust the size of the recess on the underside of the stamp body. Accordingly, this adjustment must also be taken into account during the expansion of the base area. If, on the other hand, the stamp relief and the stamp body are created at the same time, we assume that they are also produced in one piece and the need for adjustment is eliminated.

The main body of the stamp is created using a *hull* transformation, from which the relief recess is then subtracted using a Boolean difference:

```
module stamp( /* ... */ ) {
    /* ... */
    module stamp_body() {
        /* ... */

        // main body
        difference() {
            hull(){
                translate( [0, 0, body_z_null] )
                linear_extrude( height = body_base )
                base();

                translate( [0, 0, body_z_null + body_height] )
                linear_extrude( height = 0.01 )
                base( body_taper );
            }

            translate( [0, 0, stamp_depth] )
            linear_extrude( height = stamp_relief_depth)
            offset(
                delta = stamp_margin +
                        (border ? border_thickness : 0) +
                        (stamp_relief ? 0 : body_allowance)
            )
            text_area();
        }
    }
    /* ... */
}
```

The lower part of the main body consists of a *base* with height *body_base*. This creates a small edge. The upper part consists of a base reduced by *body_taper*, that is only a hundredth of a millimeter thick. This part serves only as a "lid", while the side walls are created by the *hull* transformation. The recess for the stamp relief is created directly based on the *text_area*, brought to the right size with *offset*, positioned analogous to the base of the stamp relief and finally subtracted from the main body using a Boolean difference operation.

The only thing missing now is the stamp handle:

```
module stamp( /* ... */ ) {
    /* ... */
    module stamp_body() {
        /* ... */

        // handle sphere
        translate( [0, 0, body_z_null + body_height + body_handle_height])
        sphere(d = body_handle_dm, $fn = 50);

        // handle front indicator
        color("Silver")
        translate([
            0,
            body_handle_dm / 2,
            body_z_null + body_height + body_handle_height
        ])
        scale( [1, 0.5, 1] )
        sphere(d = body_handle_ind, $fn = 25);

        // handle neck
        translate( [0, 0, body_z_null + body_height])
        rotate_extrude( $fn = 50)
        difference() {
            square(
                [body_handle_dm / 2 - body_handle_collar, body_handle_height]
            );

            translate([body_handle_dm / 2, body_handle_height / 2 ])
            scale( [0.4, 1] )
            circle( d = body_handle_height, $fn = 50 );
        }
    }
    /* ... */
}
```

The stamp handle consists of a ball, a neck underneath, and a tactile indicator that marks the front of the stamp. The ball consists of a suitably shifted *sphere* base shape.

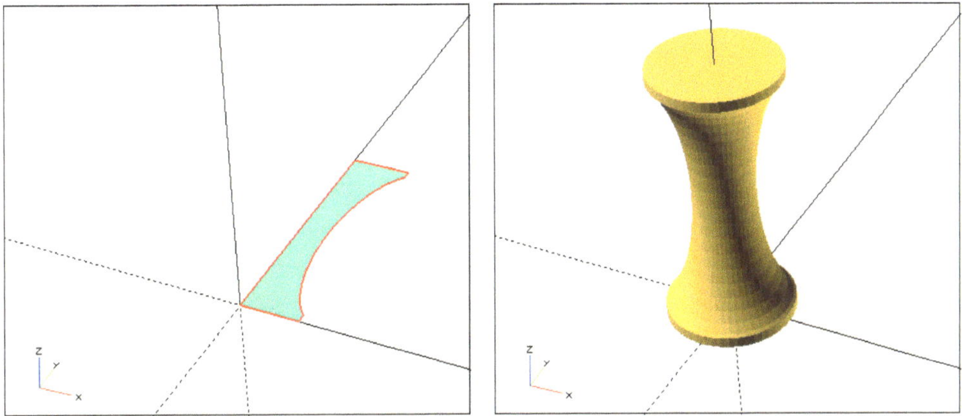

Figure 9.5: Modeling of the stamp neck by means of a rotational extrusion

The front indicator consists of a small sphere, which we have additionally compressed to 50% in the Y-direction using the *scale* transformation. We describe the neck via a rotate extrude transform (Figure 9.5). For this, we take a rectangle as 2D base shape and cut out a compressed circle on one side of the rectangle using a Boolean difference. Finally, we use a *rotate_extrude* transform to turn this 2D geometry into a concave, three-dimensional neck.

Our stamp module is now almost finished. We only have to consider the parameters *stamp_relief* and *stamp_body* when instantiating the submodules:

```
module stamp( /* ... */ ) {
    /* ... */
    if (stamp_relief) {
        color("Peru")
        rotate([0, stamp_body ? 0 : 180, 0])
        relief();
    }

    if (stamp_body) {
        stamp_body();
    }
}
```

In case of the stamp relief, we have added a rotate transform that ensures that the relief is flipped over should it be rendered on its own. This facilitates subsequent 3D printing of the relief.

A small tip at the end: If we want to use special Unicode characters in our text, we can encode them using OpenSCAD's *chr* function. The "opposite direction" is the *ord* function. It returns the corresponding Unicode for a given character. Since many fonts also contain symbols as characters, it can be an easy way to use these symbols within OpenSCAD as 2D basic shapes. For example, `text( chr( 9786 ) );` returns a smiling face as 2D geometry :).

9.3   OpenSCAD in the Command Line

We have managed to describe the stamp geometry in such a way that it automatically adapts to the dimension of the respective text. This makes the *stamp* module quite suitable to be used as an example for automated geometry creation via the command line. Such an approach could be used to offer the creation of custom stamps via an alternative interface.

In order to automatically generate stamps from the command line, our stamp instance must be parameterized within the `.scad` file using variables:

```
/* ... */

st  = "OpenSCAD";
stg = 10;

stamp(st,stg);
```

The variables must be initialized with sample values and must not remain undefined. If these conditions are met we can set these variables from the command line:

```
$ OpenSCAD -o stamp.stl -D 'st="3D-Printing!"' -D 'stg=15' stamp.scad
```

The option `-o stamp.stl` specifies the output file. The option `-D 'st="3D printing!"'` sets the variable *st* to the value "3D printing" and the option `-D 'stg=15` sets the parameter *stg* to 15. The last argument `stamp.scad` is the name of the .scad file containing our module *stamp* and the stamp instance parameterized with the variables *st* and *stg*.

Project 7: Flame Sculpture

In the majority of cases, OpenSCAD is used for the design and geometric description of technical systems or components. However, this does not mean that organic shapes could not also be created with OpenSCAD. In this project we will create a flame sculpture that we will model using a number of mathematical functions.

10.1   What's new?

In this project we will learn more about mathematical functions available in OpenSCAD (*exp*, *norm*, *cross*) and we will also create our own functions. In this context we will define a *recursive* function for the first time. Furthermore we will see how we can cascade the *children* call over several module levels and learn what the *concat* command is all about.

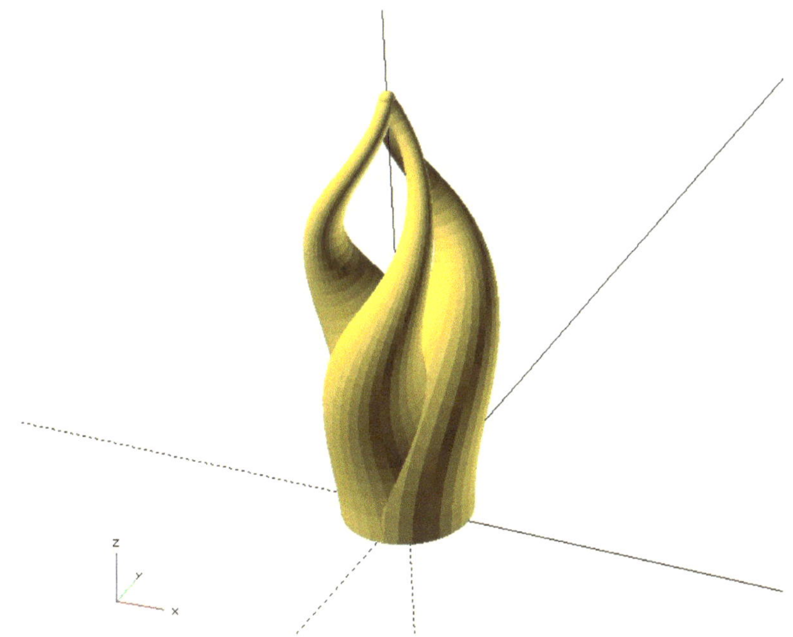

Figure 10.1: A mathematically modeled flame sculpture

10.2 Let's go

Let's start with the module description and test instance of our module. Unlike with the previous projects, we will define all parameters right at the beginning and not introduce them bit by bit:

```
// a flame sculpture

module flames(
    height,
    scaling_start     = [1.0, 1.0, 1.0],
    scaling_end       = [0.1, 0.1, 0.1],
    x_radius          = 15,
    y_radius          = 10,
    steepness         = 0.2,
    transition        = 0.35,
    height_distortion = 0.7,
    turns             = 1,
    slices            = 30
) {


}

flames(180) {
    circle( d = 60 , $fn = 30);
    sphere( d = 60 );
}
```

If you look at the test instance of our module *flames* below the module description, you will see that the module will operate on a geometry set. Doing so allows us to subsequently change the underlying geometries and thus modify the character of our sculpture.

The basic idea for our model is to first compute a set of positions describing a curved path and then move a 2D basic shape along this path and transform it into a 3D geometry by using the *hull* transformation in a pairwise fashion. In addition, the underlying 2D basic shape will be scaled along the path. Let's start with the generation of the curved path:

```
module flames(
    height,
    scaling_start    = [1.0, 1.0, 1.0],
    scaling_end      = [0.1, 0.1, 0.1],
    x_radius         = 15,
    y_radius         = 10,
    steepness        = 0.2,
    transition       = 0.35,
    height_distortion = 0.7,
    turns            = 1,
    slices           = 30
) {

    // positions along the path
    increment = height / slices;

    rot_inc = 360 * turns / slices;

    positions = [ for (i = [0:slices]) [
        cos( i * rot_inc) * x_radius,
        sin( i * rot_inc) * y_radius,
        pow( i / slices, height_distortion) * height
    ]];

}
```

The parameter *height* specifies the height of the path we want to create. The parameter *slices* specifies the number of steps we want to calculate along the path. From this we can determine an *increment* as an internal variable, which we will need later. Analogously, we derive a rotation increment *rot_inc*. We store the positions along our path as three-dimensional vectors within an array. We compute the array using a generative for-loop. Here, the X- and Y-coordinates of our positions move along an elliptical circular path with radii *x_radius* and *y_radius* while the Z-coordinate moves upwards. Instead of letting the Z-coordinate grow linearly, we use a power function to be able to influence the distribution of points along the Z-axis with the parameter *height_distortion*. Figure 10.2 gives an impression of how the power function behaves for different values of the parameter *height_distortion*.

Besides positioning, we also want to scale our basic shape along the path. Instead of scaling linearly we will use a sigmoid function. Since OpenSCAD does not offer a "ready-made" sigmoid function, we have to create one ourselves:

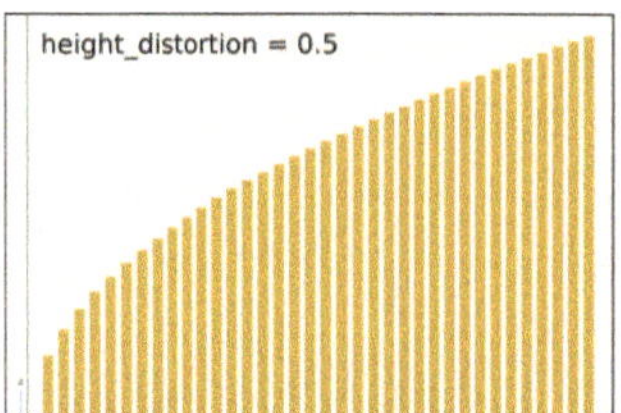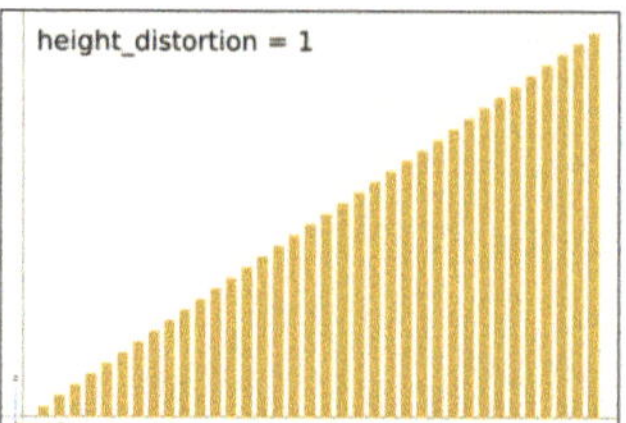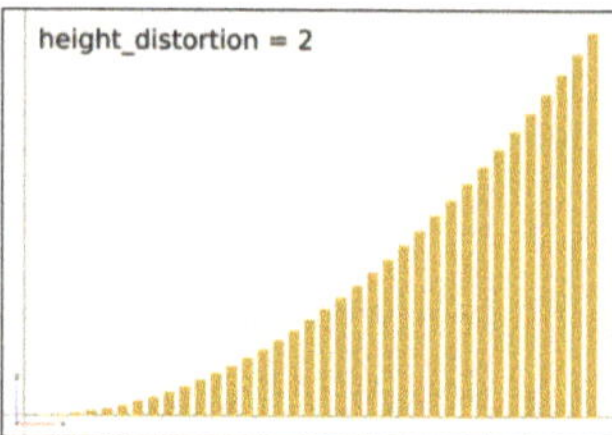

Figure 10.2: Height distortion based on power function

```
module flames(
    height,
    scaling_start     = [1.0, 1.0, 1.0],
    scaling_end       = [0.1, 0.1, 0.1],
    x_radius          = 15,
    y_radius          = 10,
    steepness         = 0.2,
    transition        = 0.35,
    height_distortion = 0.7,
    turns             = 1,
    slices            = 30
) {

    // positions along the path
    /* ... */

    // scaling along the path
    function sigmoid(x, steepness = 0.5, transition = 0.5) =
        let (
            increment       = 1.0 - pow( steepness, 0.1),
            starting_point = -transition / increment
        ) 1 / ( 1 + exp( -( x / increment + starting_point) ) );

    s_factors = [ for (i = [0:slices])
        1.0 - sigmoid( i / slices, steepness, transition )
    ];

}
```

We define our sigmoid function by means of the exponential function *exp* and the well-known scheme 1 / (1 + exp(-x)). In addition, we parameterize our function in such a way that the sigmoidal transition lies in the interval 0 to 1 of the parameter x. Furthermore, we scale the function so that we can set the relative position and slope of

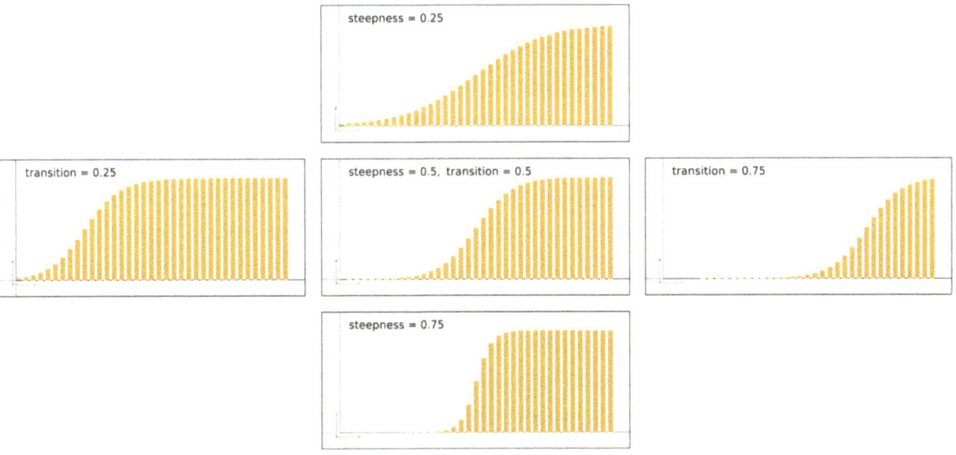

Figure 10.3: Normalized sigmoid function

the sigmoidal transition by means of the parameters *steepness* and *transition*. These two parameters also expect values between 0 and 1. Figure 10.3 gives an impression of the effect different values for *steepness* and *transition* have on the output of the function.

Like the positions, we calculate the scaling factors using a generative for-loop and store them in the *s_factors* array. Before we continue, let's create a temporary version of a single flame to see if we are on the right track:

```
module flames(
    /* ... */
    scaling_start    = [1.0, 1.0, 1.0],
    scaling_end      = [0.1, 0.1, 0.1],
    /* ... */
) {

    // positions along the path
    // scaling along the path
    /* ... */

    // a single flame
    module flame() {

        for (i = [1:slices])
        translate( positions[i] )
        linear_extrude( height = 2 )
        scale(
            scaling_start * s_factors[i] +
```

```
            scaling_end * (1.0 - s_factors[i])
        )
        children(0);

    }

    flame() children(0); // debug
}

flames( 180 ) {
    circle( d = 60 , $fn = 30);
    sphere( d = 60 );
}
```

We define a submodule *flame* and inside this module we use a single for-loop to go through the *positions* array and the *s_ factors* array in parallel and use their values to scale and translate the 2D geometry. We create the actual scaling vector as a linear interpolation between *scaling_ start* and *scaling_ end*, taking the interpolation ratio from the *s_ factors* array.

Between scaling and translation we perform a linear extrusion to transform the 2D geometry into a 3D geometry. As 2D geometry, we use `children(0)`, i.e. the element that follows the instance of the submodule *flame*. Below the definition of the submodule *flame* we have instantiated a test instance of the module. As subsequent element we have used `children(0)` again! This `children(0)` refers now to the element that follows the instance of the module *flames* (plural!). If we look at its instance, we see that here the first subsequent element is a circle with a diameter of 60. The chain of calls to `children()` forwards this outer element down into the submodule *flame*.

Figure 10.4 shows our intermediate result so far. The circle geometry recognizably follows a curved path and is scaled in the process. Theoretically, we could now connect the circles pairwise using the *hull* transformation and would obtain an already quite passable 3D geometry. However, it would be much nicer if the circles would tilt according to the local orientation of the path. To implement this, we need to figure out in which direction the path points at each position and then rotate the circle to match that direction. To figure that out we need some mathematics.

We get the cosine of the angle between two vectors if we divide the dot product of the two vectors by the product of the lengths of the two vectors. For the calculation of the length of a vector OpenSCAD offers the function *norm*. The calculation of the

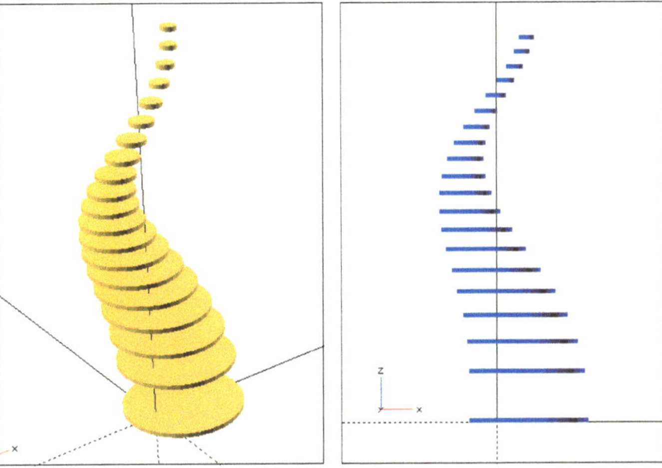

Figure 10.4: Displacement of a 2D basic shape along a path (left) and its corresponding orthogonal side view (right)

dot product we have to define ourselves. The dot product of two vectors *v1* and *v2* is calculated by multiplying the individual components of the vectors together and then summing up these products (v1[0] * v2[0] + v1[1] * v2[1] + ... + v1[n] * v2[n]). In most programming languages, we would go through the vectors one element at a time to do this, and gradually build our sum. In OpenSCAD we cannot create such a "running sum", because variables can only be assigned once. A solution to this problem is the use of recursion:

```
module flames( /* ... */ ) {

    // positions along the path
    // scaling along the path
    /* ... */

    // angles along the path
    function dot_p(v1, v2, idx) =
        v1[idx] * v2[idx] + (idx > 0 ? dot_p(v1, v2, idx-1) : 0);

    function dot_product(v1, v2) = dot_p(v1, v2, len(v1)-1);

    // a single flame
    /* ... */

}
```

The function *dot_p* calculates the dot product of two vectors *v1* and *v2* in a recursive way. To do this the function needs a third parameter *idx*. The second function *dot_product* starts the recursion. It calls *dot_p* and sets at this initial call the value of the parameter *idx* to the index of the last element (`len(v1) - 1`) of the vectors. The function *dot_p* then calculates the product of the last elements of *v1* and *v2* and, depending on the value of *idx*, adds either a 0, or the value that the **recursive** call to the function *dot_p* yields. The key part - as with all recursive functions - is to make sure that the function does not call itself infinitely often. We achieve this here by giving the parameter *idx* the value `idx - 1` when *dot_p* is called recursively. This way the value of *idx* becomes smaller with each recursive call. If it arrives at 0, no further recursive call takes place and the function is terminated. Along the way, we calculated the products of all elements and summed them up. The final result is the dot product of *v1* and *v2*. If your head is buzzing a bit now: this is a normal side effect of dealing with recursive algorithms!

Now we can use our dot product to calculate the angles along the path:

```
module flames( /* ... */ ) {

    // positions along the path
    // scaling along the path
    // angles along the path
    /* ... */



    function angle( v1, v2) = acos(dot_product(v1, v2) / (norm(v1) * norm(v2)));

    rel_pos = concat(
        [ positions[0] ],
        [ for (i = [1:slices]) positions[i] - positions[i-1] ]
    );

    pos_angles = concat(
        [0],
        [ for (i = [1:slices-1]) angle( [0,0,1], rel_pos[i]) ],
        [0]
    );

    // a single flame

    /* ... */
}
```

We first define the function *angle*, which gives us the angle between two vectors *v1* and *v2*. As described before, we divide the dot product by the product of the lengths and determine the angle via the arc cosine function. To calculate the angles along the path, we first have to determine the relative directions of the individual path segments from our absolute *positions*. To do this, we create an array *rel_pos* that we combine from two arrays using the function *concat*. The first array contains only one element: the first position of our path. The second array contains for each following position of the path the difference between this position (`positions[i]`) and the previous position (`positions[i-1]`). Accordingly, the loop variable *i* does not start at 0 but at 1 (i = `[1:levels]`). Together, we get an array *rel_pos* whose entries go from 0 to *slices*. So it is as long as the array *positions*.

Now we have completed all preparations to finally be able to define the *pos_angles* array that will contain the angles along the path. Since we don't want to rotate the first and the last 2D geometry, we compose the *pos_angles* array from three individual arrays. The first and last entries are simply set to 0. The entries in between are generated using a generative for-loop, which uses our function *angle* to calculate the angle between the vertical `[0, 0, 1]` and the respective relative path segment `rel_pos[i]`. Again, we made sure that the entries of the array *pos_angles* go from 0 to *slices*. This makes the later use of these arrays more elegant, as we can avoid some special case handling for the beginning and end of the path.

Now we can put the angle information to work in our temporary submodule *flame*:

```
module flames( /* ... */ ) {

    // positions along the path
    // scaling along the path
    // angles along the path
    /* ... */

    // a single flame
    module flame() {

        for (i = [1:slices])
        translate( positions[i] )
        rotate( pos_angles[i], cross([0,0,1], rel_pos[i]) )
        linear_extrude( height = 2 )
        scale(
```

```
                scaling_start * s_factors[i] +
                scaling_end * (1.0 - s_factors[i])
            )
        children(0);
    }


    flame() children(0); // debug


}
```

We insert a rotate transform before the translation of the basic shape. We use the special variant of the *rotate* transform, to which we can separately pass an angle and a vector around which the rotation should take place. As angle we pass the previously determined angle from the field *pos_ angles*. The rotation axis is the vector perpendicular to the vector of our relative direction *rel_ pos* and the vertical ([0, 0, 1]). This vector can be calculated by the cross product of the other two vectors. Fortunately, we do not have to implement the cross product ourselves, but can use the OpenSCAD function *cross* instead. Figure 10.5 shows what our current intermediate result looks like.

In the next step, we need to modify the *flame* submodule a bit. After all, our goal is to connect the individual geometries along the path *pairwise* with the *hull* transformation. Therefore we detach the geometry description from the for-loop and move it into another submodule *slice* that we can index with the loop variable *i*:

```
module flames( /* ... */ ) {

    // positions along the path
    // scaling along the path
    // angles along the path
    /* ... */

    // a single flame
    module flame() {

        module slice( i ) {
            translate( positions[i] )
            rotate( pos_angles[i], cross([0,0,1], rel_pos[i]) )
            linear_extrude( height = 0.01 )
            scale(
                scaling_start * s_factors[i] +
                scaling_end * (1.0 - s_factors[i])
            )
```

```
            children(0);
        }

        for (i = [1:slices])
        hull() {
            slice(i-1) children(0);
            slice(i) children(0);
        }
    }

    flame() children(0); // debug
}
```

The *slice* submodule encapsulates a single basic shape at the ith position along the path. Before, we used an extrusion length of 2 millimeters for our intermediate results. Now we reduce the extrusion length to 0.01 millimeters. This effectively brings us back to working with a 2D geometry, but allows us to manipulate it in 3D. The for-loop in the parent module *flame* connects the slices in pairs. Note that the loop variable *i* now starts from 1 instead of 0, so that we are allowed to make the statement `slice(i-1)`

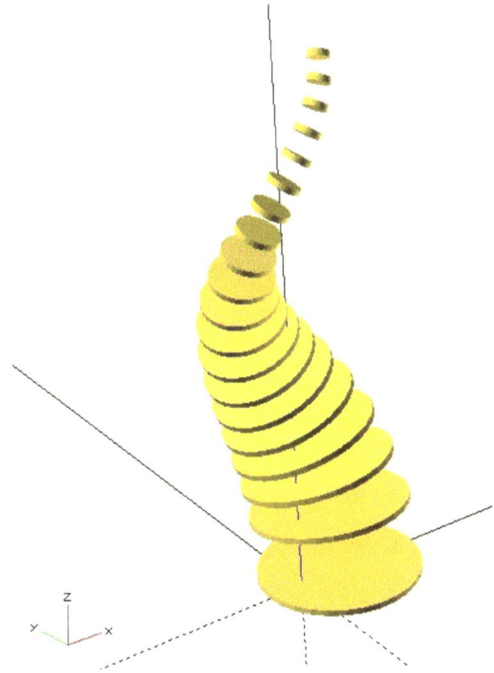

Figure 10.5: Correct rotation of the 2D base shape along the path

Figure 10.6: Pairwise connection of the basic shapes along the path using *hull* transformation

`children(0);` inside the geometry set of the *hull* transformation. As before, we need to pass the externally set geometry down into the *slice* submodule using `children(0)`.

This completes the geometry description of a single flame (Figure 10.6). What remains now is to arrange our single flame as a flame triplet. Before that, we should remove the test instance of the *flame* module (`// debug`):

```
module flames(
    /* ... */
) {

    // positions along the path
    // scaling along the path
    // angles along the path
    // a single flame
    /* ... */

    // flame triplet
    translate([-x_radius,0,0])
    union(){
        flame()
        children(0);
```

```
            translate([x_radius,0,0])
            rotate([0,0,120])
            translate([-x_radius,0,0])
            flame()
            children(0);

            translate([x_radius,0,0])
            rotate([0,0,240])
            translate([-x_radius,0,0])
            flame()
            children(0);
        }
}
```

Our flame triplet consists of a Boolean union and three flames each rotated by 120 degrees relative to each other. Since the basic shapes inside the module *flame* always start their curved circular path at [x_radius, 0], we have to move the flames temporarily back to the origin before rotating them.

In its current form, the flame triplet ends up with a blunt tip. To improve the situation, we position a suitably scaled cap at the tip of the triplet. The geometry for this cap is supplied as the second element (`children(1);`) of the external geometry set:

```
module flames(
    /* ... */
){
    // positions along the path
    // scaling along the path
    // angles along the path
    // a single flame
    // flame triplet
    /* ... */

    // end cap
    if ($children > 1) {
        translate([-x_radius,0,0])
        translate(positions[len(positions)-1])
        scale(
            scaling_start * s_factors[len(s_factors)-1] +
            scaling_end * (1.0 - s_factors[len(s_factors)-1])
        )
        children(1);
    }
}
```

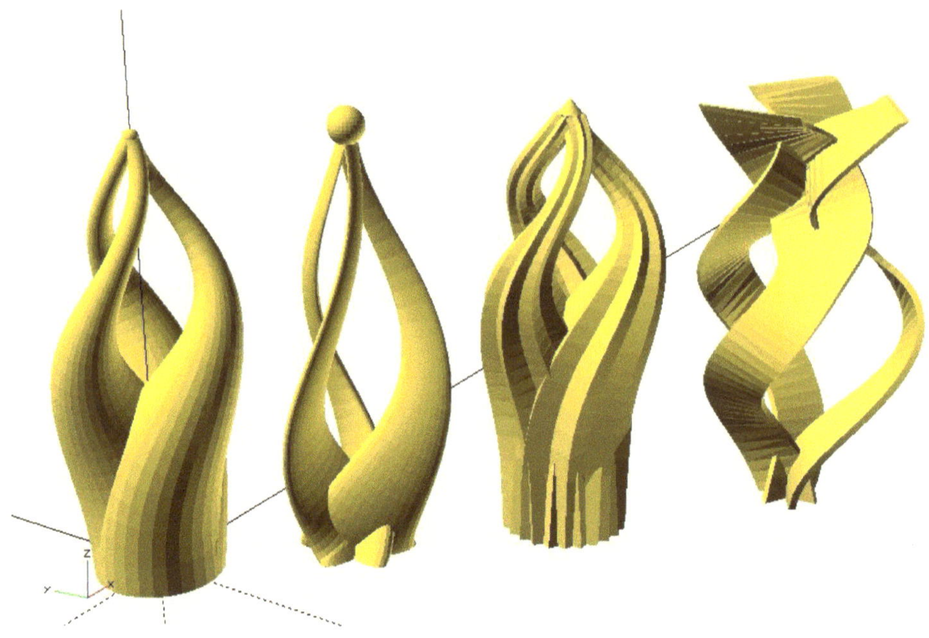

Figure 10.7: Flame sculpture variations

Our geometry description is now complete! The approach of defining both the 2D base shape and the geometry of the final cap via an external geometry set makes it easy to customize our flame sculpture. In addition, the different parameters of the module offer a number of further options for influencing the overall shape of the flame.

10.3   Flame Sculpture Variations

Figure 10.7 shows a number of variants created by just changing the supplied geometries and parameters.

Here are the associated instantiations of the variants in figure 10.7:

```
// Number 1
flames( 180 ) {
    circle( d = 60 , $fn = 30);
    sphere( d = 60 );
}
```

```
// Number 2
translate( [60, -60, 0] )
flames(
    180,
    steepness         = 0.1,
    transition        = 0.3,
    height_distortion = 1.2,
    slices            = 30
) {
    scale( [1, 0.33] )
    circle( d = 60 , $fn = 30);
    sphere( d = 120 );
}

// Number 3
union(){
    translate( [125, -125, 0] )
    flames(
        180,
        scaling_start     = [1.0, 1.0, 1.0],
        scaling_end       = [0.2, 0.2, 0.2],
        steepness         = 0.3,
        transition        = 0.35,
        height_distortion = 0.5,
        slices            = 30
    ) {
        square( 40, center = true);
        cylinder( d1 = 50, d2 = 0, h = 30);
    }

    translate( [125, -125, 0] )
    flames(
        180,
        scaling_start     = [1.0, 1.0, 1.0],
        scaling_end       = [0.2, 0.2, 0.2],
        steepness         = 0.3,
        transition        = 0.35,
        height_distortion = 0.5,
        slices            = 30
    ) {
        rotate( [0, 0, 45] )
        square( 40, center = true);
        cylinder( d1 = 50, d2 = 0, h = 30);
    }
}
```

```
// Number 4
translate( [200, -200, 0] )
flames(
    180,
    scaling_start     = [0.6, 0.6, 1.0],
    scaling_end       = [0.4, 1.0, 1.0],
    x_radius          = 25,
    y_radius          = 15,
    steepness         = 0.8,
    transition        = 0.6,
    height_distortion = 0.8,
    turns = 1.3,
    slices            = 50
) {
    square( [5, 45], center = true);
}
```

Project 8: Recursive Tree

Natural structures, such as the shape of plants, often arise from growth processes that are based on relatively simple rules. By means of recursive geometry descriptions we can reproduce such growth processes in a simplified form and generate complex geometries that resemble these natural structures. In this project, we want to reproduce the appearance of a tree using such a recursive geometry description.

11.1   What's new?

We have already seen that recursive functions can be used to define iterative algorithms in OpenSCAD. Here we will learn about the possibility to use recursion also in the geometry description itself. Furthermore, we will see how to generate random numbers using the *rands* function.

Figure 11.1: A tree generated from a recursive geometry description

11.2 Let's go

A warning must be given right at the beginning: recursive geometries can grow very quickly in their complexity and bring practically every computer system very quickly to its respective limits. Especially the so-called *recursion depth*, which is a parameter of every recursive geometry description, is crucial in this regard. In the following design, you should change this parameter only with extreme caution.

The basic idea for our recursive tree is to let the tree grow step by step as in a growth process. Each step will be recursive. Let's start with a minimal geometry description:

```
module r_tree(
    h_increment,
    main_depth,
){
    linear_extrude( height = h_increment )
    children(0);

    if (main_depth > 0) {

        translate( [0, 0, h_increment] )
        r_tree(
            h_increment,
            main_depth - 1
        ) {
            children(0);
        }
    }
}

r_tree(
    h_increment = 10,
    main_depth  = 20
) {
    circle( d = 10, $fn=8);
}
```

The module *r_tree* has two parameters *h_increment* and *main_depth* so far. The *h_increment* sets the height by which we want to grow each step. The *main_depth* specifies how many more steps we can go in the current section of the tree. Inside the module, we first create a piece of the tree using linear extrusion of the 2D geometry passed to the module. Then we check if we have any more growth steps left (if (main_depth > 0) ...). If so, we recursively use the module *r_tree* as a geometry that is shifted up by *h_increment*. This *recursive* usage basically copies the module description of the module *r_tree* to that location in the description again. This is a bit like the effect of looking into two opposing mirrors resulting in an endless sequence of copies.

To prevent that this sequence of copies in our module description becomes endless, the parameter *main_depth* is key. In the recursive definition of *r_tree*, we reduce *main_depth* by 1. This way, *main_depth* becomes slightly smaller with each step, until finally *main_depth* takes the value 0 and the copying stops. In addition, we forward the outer geometry passed to our module to the recursive copy by appending `children(0)`.

Next, we want to create some random variations in our module description. We can do this by using the *rands* function:

```
module r_tree(
    h_increment,
    main_depth,
    rnd_seed
){
    rnd_values = rands( 0, 1, 10, rnd_seed );

    linear_extrude( height = h_increment )
    children(0);

    if (main_depth > 0) {

        translate( [0, 0, h_increment] )
        r_tree(
            h_increment,
            main_depth - 1 - rnd_values[0] * 2,
            rnd_values[9] * 100
        ) {
            children(0);
        }
    }
}

r_tree(
    h_increment = 10,
    main_depth  = 20,
    rnd_seed    = 42
) {
    circle( d = 10, $fn=8);
}
```

The function *rands* (short for *random values*) creates an array of random numbers. The first two parameters specify the lower and upper bound of these numbers. In our case we generate random decimal numbers between 0 and 1. The third parameter specifies how many random numbers the array should contain. We let *rands* generate 10 numbers for now, since we'll be sprinkling in "randomness" at various points within our module. The last parameter is an initialization value that we define externally via the module parameter *rnd_seed*. The random numbers generated by the *rands* function are not really random. They only look like that. In reality, they are just pseudo-random numbers that have a fixed order. The initialization value (an arbitrary number), determines this order. This has the advantage that with different initialization values we get different sequences of random numbers, but at the same time we keep control over the random sequences. If we do not change the initialization value, we always get the same sequence of numbers. Specifically, for our tree, this means that we can change the *rnd_seed* parameter of our module to generate a new tree variant. If we like the variant, we can remember the value of *rnd_seed* and thus recreate the respective variant. If this would not be the case and the random numbers were truly random, we would get a different tree every time we computed the geometry.

In our module *r_tree* we use the random numbers in two places. First, we reduce the *main_depth* in the recursive definition of *r_tree* not only by one, but also by a random value between 0 and 2 (`random[0] * 2`). For this we use the first of our ten random numbers. Second, we pass the last of our ten random numbers to the recursive instance as a new *rnd_seed* value. We scale the value to a range between 0 and 100, since the documentation of *rands* is a bit unclear whether it requires integers or decimal values for initialization. By scaling the number we're just playing it safe here. If you now change the value of *rnd_seed* in the test instance of the module *r_tree* and run a preview (*F5*), you will see how the height of our "tree" changes randomly with each value of *rnd_seed*.

The trunk and branches of trees are predominantly straight, but do show variations in their thickness and become thinner in the direction of growth. We can model this via a scaling parameter:

```
module r_tree(
    h_increment,
    main_depth,
    rnd_seed,
    scaling,
    s_variance
){
    rnd_values = rands( 0, 1, 10, rnd_seed );

    function z(from, to, idx) = rnd_values[idx] * (to - from) + from;

    sf = scaling + z(-1, 1 ,1) * s_variance;

    linear_extrude( height = h_increment, scale = sf )
    children(0);

    if (main_depth > 0) {

        translate( [0, 0, h_increment] )
        r_tree(
            h_increment,
            main_depth - 1 - z(0,2,0),
            z(0,100,9),
            scaling,
            s_variance
        ) {
            scale( [sf, sf] )
            children(0);
        }
    }
}

r_tree(
    h_increment = 10,
    main_depth  = 20,
    rnd_seed    = 42,
    scaling     = 0.97,
    s_variance  = 0.1
) {
    circle( d = 10, $fn=8);
}
```

We have added two new parameters to our module *r_tree*. The parameter *scaling* specifies to what percentage the passed basic shape should shrink in each step. The parameter *s_variance* sets the random variation of the *scaling*. Inside the module, we first cleaned it up a bit and defined a function *z* that gives us a random value from the *random* array and scales it to an interval `[from,to]`. This makes further use of random numbers in our module a bit more convenient. Next, we determine a scaling factor *sf* from the parameters *scaling* and *s_variance* that is applied to the current step of the recursion. We pass *sf* to the linear extrusion (*linear_extrude*) as parameter *scale*. To ensure that the next tree section now neatly connects to the scaled basic shape, we have to scale it accordingly (`scale( [sf, sf] )`) when passing it to the recursive usage of *r_tree*.

Our tree is currently nothing more than a single branch. To change this, we need to fork (at least) one branch at some point during our simulated growth process. To prevent us from branching infinitely often, we need to introduce another recursion depth variable *branch_depth* for this new *recursion path*:

```
module r_tree(
    h_increment,
    md_init,
    main_depth,
    rnd_seed,
    scaling,
    s_variance,
    bd_init,
    branch_depth,
    branch_angle
){
    /* ... */
    linear_extrude( height = h_increment, scale = sf )
    children(0);

    // should we branch?
    if (
        (branch_depth > 0) &&
        (z(0, 0.8 ,2) < ((md_init - main_depth) / md_init) )
    ){
        r_angle  = z(0, 720, 3);
        br_angle = branch_angle / 2 + z(0, 0.5, 4) * branch_angle;

        translate( [0, 0, h_increment] )
        rotate( [0, 0, r_angle] )
        rotate( [br_angle, 0, 0] )
        r_tree(
            h_increment,
            md_init,
```

```
                main_depth,
                z(0,100, 5),
                scaling,
                s_variance,
                bd_init,
                branch_depth - 1,
                branch_angle
            ) {
                scale( [sf, sf] )
                children(0);
            }
        }

    if (main_depth > 0) {

        translate( [0, 0, h_increment] )
        r_tree(
            h_increment,
            md_init,
            main_depth - 1 - z(0,2,0),
            z(0,100, 9),
            scaling,
            s_variance,
            bd_init,
            branch_depth,
            branch_angle
        ) {
            scale( [sf, sf] )
            children(0);
        }
    }
    }
}

r_tree(
    h_increment  = 10,
    md_init      = 20,
    main_depth   = 20,
    rnd_seed     = 42,
    scaling      = 0.97,
    s_variance   = 0.1,
    bd_init      = 1,
    branch_depth = 1,
    branch_angle = 30
) {
    circle( d = 10, $fn=8);
}
```

We have extended our module *r_tree* by some parameters. The two init parameters *md_init* and *bd_init* contain the initial values of the parameters *main_depth* and *branch_depth*. We need these initial values to be able to start "fresh" with a new branch in case of a fork. In addition, we have introduced the parameter *branch_angle*, with which we define the (maximum) angle of the branching process.

After the geometry description of our current branch section (`linear_extrude` ...), we decide whether a new branch should break off at this point. We do this only if two conditions are met: the *branch_depth* must be greater than 0 (*safe recursion end!*) **and** (`&&`) a random value between 0 and 0.8 must be smaller than a certain ratio between the current main depth and the initial main depth (`(md_init - main_depth) / md_init`). Why is that? Let's put in some numbers to see how the ratio changes over time. At the beginning, the current *main_depth* is equal to the initial main depth *md_init*. This makes the ratio 0. That a random value from the interval 0 to 0.8 is smaller than 0 is impossible. At the end, the current *main_depth* is 0. Then the ratio becomes 1. In this case, it is guaranteed that a random value from the interval 0 to 0.8 is smaller. In other words, the further our branch grows, the more likely it is that a new branch will be forked.

Inside the if-statement we first define two angles *r_angle* and *br_angle*. The rotation angle *r_angle* is a random angle that determines in which direction the branch should branch off. The branch angle *br_angle* determines the concrete branch angle of the branch as a mixture of the parameter *branch_angle* and a random part. Subsequently, the new branch is described by recursively using the module *r_tree*, which is now rotated before being shifted by *h_increment*. The *main_depth* of this new branch is reset to

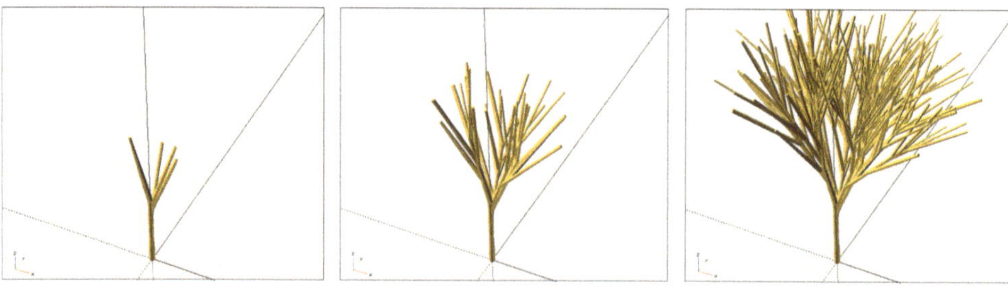

Figure 11.2: Effect of the parameter *branch_depth* for values of 1, 2 and 3

md_init. The *branch_depth*, on the other hand, is decreased by 1. Figure 11.2 shows the effect of this second recursion path for recursion depths of 1, 2, and 3.

Our branches seem a bit unrealistically long at the moment, and they do kind of pile up unnaturally depending on chance. Let's address the first problem by assuming that the height increment should decrease as the recursion depth increases. We can make this possible via another parameter *r_decrement* for the increment reduction:

```
module r_tree(
    h_increment,
    r_decrement,
    md_init,
    main_depth,
    rnd_seed,
    scaling,
    s_variance,
    bd_init,
    branch_depth,
    branch_angle
){
    /* ... */

    // should we branch?
    if (
        (branch_depth > 0) &&
        (z(0, 0.8 ,2) < ((md_init - main_depth) / md_init) )
    ){
        r_angle = z(0, 720, 3);
        br_angle = branch_angle / 2 + z(0, 0.5, 4) * branch_angle;

        new_increment =
            h_increment -
            h_increment / 2.5 * pow(r_decrement, branch_depth);

        translate( [0, 0, h_increment] )
        rotate( [0, 0, r_angle] )
        rotate( [br_angle, 0, 0] )
        r_tree(
            new_increment,
            r_decrement,
            md_init,
            md_init,
            z(0,100, 5),
            scaling,
            s_variance,
```

```
                    bd_init,
                    branch_depth - 1,
                    branch_angle
            ) {
                scale( [sf, sf] )
                children(0);
            }
        }

    if (main_depth > 0) {

            translate( [0, 0, h_increment] )
            r_tree(
                h_increment,
                r_decrement,
                md_init,
                main_depth - 1 - z(0,2,0),
                z(0,100,9),
                scaling,
                s_variance,
                bd_init,
                branch_depth,
                branch_angle
            ) {
                scale( [sf, sf] )
                children(0);
            }
        }
}

r_tree(
    h_increment = 10,
    r_decrement = 0.7,
    /* ... */
) {
    circle( d = 10, $fn=8);
}
```

We use a power function for the decrease of the height increment. Since *r_decrement* is less than 1, higher powers make the resulting value smaller. In other words: with increasing recursion depth the reduction of the height increment increases.

Make sure that you update the parameter lists at all occurrences of the module *r_tree*. Unfortunately, due to a bug in OpenSCAD, we cannot set default values for the parameters and have to specify them **completely** each time. If you try to use default parameters, OpenSCAD crashes with a memory error after a certain number of parameters.

Now we can take care of the second problem. The forked branches start with the same size as the branch from which they emerge. This is not very realistic. The size of the forked branch should be smaller and also depend on its angle. If the angle is large, the diameter should be rather small. In addition, the main branch should also lose some of its diameter and, depending on the angle of the forked branch, should give way to it somewhat. Let us convert these thoughts into a geometry description:

```
module r_tree(
    h_increment,
    r_decrement,
    md_init,
    main_depth,
    rnd_seed,
    scaling,
    s_variance,
    bd_init,
    branch_depth,
    branch_angle,
    branch_min_size,
    branch_max_size
){
    /* ... */

    // should we branch?
    if (
        (branch_depth > 0) &&
        (z(0, 0.8 ,2) < ((md_init - main_depth) / md_init) )
    ){
        /* ... */

        // goes to 0, if br_angle is large
        // goes to 1, if br_angle is small
        branch_ratio = (branch_angle / br_angle) - 1.0;

        branch_scaling =
            branch_min_size * branch_ratio +
            branch_max_size * (1.0 - branch_ratio);

        main_scaling =
            sf * branch_ratio +
            branch_max_size * (1.0 - branch_ratio);
```

```
            translate( [0, 0, h_increment] )
            rotate( [0, 0, r_angle] )
            rotate( [br_angle, 0, 0] )
            r_tree(
                new_increment,
                r_decrement,
                md_init,
                md_init,
                z(0,100, 5),
                scaling,
                s_variance,
                bd_init,
                branch_depth - 1,
                branch_angle,
                branch_min_size,
                branch_max_size
            ) {
                scale( [branch_scaling, branch_scaling] )
                children(0);
            }

            // main path rotated in counter-direction
            if (main_depth > 0) {
                translate( [0, 0, h_increment] )
                rotate( [0, 0, r_angle] )
                rotate( [-(branch_angle - br_angle), 0, 0] )
                r_tree(
                    new_increment,
                    r_decrement,
                    md_init,
                    main_depth - 1 - z(0,2, 6),
                    z(0,100, 7),
                    scaling,
                    s_variance,
                    bd_init,
                    branch_depth,
                    branch_angle,
                    branch_min_size,
                    branch_max_size
                ) {
                    scale( [main_scaling, main_scaling] )
                    children(0);
                }
            }
```

```openscad
    } else {

        if (main_depth > 0) {
            translate( [0, 0, h_increment] )
            r_tree(
                h_increment,
                r_decrement,
                md_init,
                main_depth - 1 - z(0,2,0),
                z(0,100,9),
                scaling,
                s_variance,
                bd_init,
                branch_depth,
                branch_angle,
                branch_min_size,
                branch_max_size
            ) {
                scale( [sf, sf] )
                children(0);
            }
        }
    }
}

r_tree(
    /* ... */
    branch_min_size = 0.3,
    branch_max_size = 0.8
) {
    circle( d = 10, $fn=8);
}
```

The geometry description has become a lot more extensive! We have added two new parameters *branch_ min_ size* and *branch_ max_ size*. These determine the size range of forked branches in relation to the size of the main branch. Inside the module, we have moved the case where we do not branch into an *else* block. This means that in the case of branching, we do not continue growing straight ahead with the main branch but stop the normal growth.

Within the description of the branch, we first determine a *branch_ ratio* and use this to define new scaling factors for both the forked branch and the main branch (*branch_ scaling* and *main_ scaling*). In the subsequent definition of the forked branch, *branch_ scaling* is then used to scale the forwarded **children(0)** geometry. After the definition of the

Figure 11.3: Gaps and hard edges between tree slices at branch points

forked branch follows a new definition of the main branch. Here, too, it is first checked whether the main branch should be continued at all (`if (main_depth > 0)`). In contrast to the normal main branch growth, the main branch is now rotated away from the forked branch (`rotate( [-(branch_angle - br_angle), 0, 0] )`) and the geometry of the continued main branch is scaled by *main_scaling*. In addition, the main branch now also adopts the *new_increment* value of the forked branch. If you set *bd_init* and *branch_depth* to 3 or even 4 as a test, you can see that we are on the right track.

If you look closely, you can see that the junctions at the branch points still look very rough (Figure 11.3). We can solve this with the help of *hull* transformations:

```
module r_tree( /* ... */ ) {
    /* ... */
    // should we branch?
    if (
        (branch_depth > 0) &&
        (z(0, 0.8 ,2) < ((md_init - main_depth) / md_init) )
    ){
        /* ... */
        translate( [0, 0, h_increment] )
        rotate( [0, 0, r_angle] )
        rotate( [br_angle, 0, 0] )
        r_tree( /* ... */ ) {
            scale( [branch_scaling, branch_scaling] )
            children(0);
        }
```

```
// smooth out connection to branching path
hull() {
    translate( [0, 0, h_increment] )
    linear_extrude( height = 0.01 )
    scale([sf,sf])
    children(0);

    translate( [0, 0, h_increment] )
    rotate( [0, 0, r_angle] )
    rotate( [br_angle, 0, 0] )
    linear_extrude(
        height = new_increment / 2,
        scale = pow(scaling,1/3)
    )
    scale( [branch_scaling, branch_scaling] )
    children(0);
}

// main path rotated in counter-direction
if (main_depth > 0) {
    translate( [0, 0, h_increment] )
    rotate( [0, 0, r_angle] )
    rotate( [-(branch_angle - br_angle), 0, 0] )
    r_tree( /* ... */ ) {
        scale( [main_scaling, main_scaling] )
        children(0);
    }

    // smooth out connection to main path
    hull() {
        translate( [0, 0, h_increment] )
        linear_extrude( height = 0.01 )
        scale([sf,sf])
        children(0);

        translate( [0, 0, h_increment] )
        rotate( [0, 0, r_angle] )
        rotate( [-(branch_angle - br_angle), 0, 0] )
        linear_extrude(
            height = new_increment / 2,
            scale = pow(scaling,1/3)
        )
        scale( [main_scaling, main_scaling] )
        children(0);
    }
}
```

```
    } else {

        if (main_depth > 0) {
            translate( [0, 0, h_increment] )
            r_tree(
                h_increment,
                r_decrement,
                md_init,
                main_depth - 1 - z(0,2,0),
                z(0,100,9),
                scaling,
                s_variance,
                bd_init,
                branch_depth,
                branch_angle,
                branch_min_size,
                branch_max_size
            ) {
                scale( [sf, sf] )
                children(0);
            }
        }
    }
}

r_tree(
    h_increment     = 10,
    r_decrement     = 0.7,
    md_init         = 20,
    main_depth      = 20,
    rnd_seed        = 42,
    scaling         = 0.97,
    s_variance      = 0.1,
    bd_init         = 1,
    branch_depth    = 1,
    branch_angle    = 30,
    branch_min_size = 0.3,
    branch_max_size = 0.8
) {
    circle( d = 10, $fn=8);
}
```

For smoothing the junctions we instantiate the outer geometry (*children(0)*) twice. We position one instance at the end of the current growth section and the other instance at the beginning of the branch or at the beginning of the rotated main branch. We give the latter instance half the height of the next growth section and scale it accordingly. Then

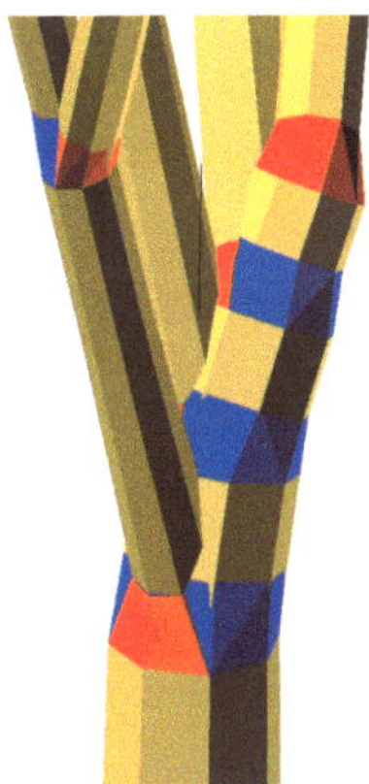

Figure 11.4: The gaps between the tree slices at branch points are now closed (branches red, main branches blue)

we use the *hull* transformation to connect both "tree slices" and thus bridge the existing gaps (Figure 11.4).

What we are still missing are the leaves of the tree. We can use the branch depth to draw leaves instead of a branch in the last recursion step:

```
module r_tree( /* ... */ ) {

    rnd_values = rands( 0, 1, 10, rnd_seed );

    function z(from, to, idx) = rnd_values[idx] * (to - from) + from;

    if ((branch_depth < 1) && ($children > 1)) {

        color("green")
        rotate([(floor(rnd_seed) % 2 == 0) ? 45 : -45,0,0])
        linear_extrude(height = 0.1)
        children(1);

    } else {

        /* ... */

        // should we branch?
        if (
            (branch_depth > 0) &&
            (z(0, 0.8 ,2) < ((md_init - main_depth) / md_init) )
        ){
```

```
        /* ... */

        translate( [0, 0, h_increment] )
        rotate( [0, 0, r_angle] )
        rotate( [br_angle, 0, 0] )
        r_tree( /* ... */ ) {
            scale( [branch_scaling, branch_scaling] )
            children(0);
            if ($children > 1) children(1);
        }

        // smooth out connection to branching path
        /* ... */

        // main path rotated in counter-direction
        if (main_depth > 0) {
            translate( [0, 0, h_increment] )
            rotate( [0, 0, r_angle] )
            rotate( [-(branch_angle - br_angle), 0, 0] )
            r_tree( /* ... */ ) {
                scale( [main_scaling, main_scaling] )
                children(0);
                if ($children > 1) children(1);
            }

            // smooth out connection to main path
            /* ... */
        }

    } else {

        if (main_depth > 0) {
            translate( [0, 0, h_increment] )
            r_tree( /* ... */ ) {
                scale( [sf, sf] )
                children(0);
                if ($children > 1) children(1);
            }
        }

        if ((branch_depth < 2) && ($children > 1)) {

            color("green")
            rotate([[(floor(rnd_seed) % 2 == 0) ? 45 : -45,0,0])
            linear_extrude(height = 0.1)
            children(1);
```

```
            }
        }
    }
}

r_tree(
    /* ... */
    bd_init       = 4,
    branch_depth  = 4,
    /* ... */
) {
    circle( d = 10, $fn=8);
    square([2,2]);
}
```

As leaves we use the other geometry passed to our module from outside (here: square ([2,2]);). Accordingly, we need to update all recursive uses of *r_ tree* within our module and also pass the geometry children(1) along. However, we should only do this if a second geometry was actually passed. Therefore, we check $children every time before we forward children(1). Since the yield of leaves is somewhat low if one draws the leaves only at the end of the recursion (if (branch_depth < 1)) we have defined the leaf geometry once more below the regular growth path and define it there when we are at the second to last recursion level (if (branch_depth < 2)). As we now only get a nice leaf canopy from a total recursion depth of about 4, we also adjusted the parameters of the test instance of our module *r_ tree*. The expression (floor(rnd_seed) % 2 == 0) ? 45 : -45 causes the leaves to be rotated sometimes in one direction and sometimes in the other depending on whether the rounded down (*floor*) value of *rnd_ seed* is even or odd. We have taken the value rnd_seed at this point, because it changes constantly. We could just as well have taken any other value from the random array.

With this we are done with our geometry description. If you want to automatically create some random trees, you can parameterize the test instance as follows:

```
srnd = rands(0,1000,1)[0];

echo(srnd);

r_tree(
    h_increment   = 10,
    r_decrement   = 0.7,
    md_init       = 20,
```

```
    main_depth       = 20,
    rnd_seed         = srnd,
    scaling          = 0.97,
    s_variance       = 0.1,
    bd_init          = 4,
    branch_depth     = 4,
    branch_angle     = 50,
    branch_min_size  = 0.3,
    branch_max_size  = 0.8
) {
    circle( d = 10, $fn=8);
    square([2,2]);
}
```

The variable *srnd* now contains a single random number, which we use for the parameter *rnd_ seed* of the module *r_ tree*. Since we use the *rands* function without init parameter here, we get a new random number with each preview or render (*F5* or *F6*). The *echo* command outputs the number to the OpenSCAD console. This way we can spot "good" init values that have produced nice trees. It is also worth varying the *branch_ angle* parameter. The same applies to *bd_ init* and *branch_ depth* if your patience and the available processing power of your computer allow it. Figure 11.5 shows two trees with 40 and 60 degrees branch angles respectively.

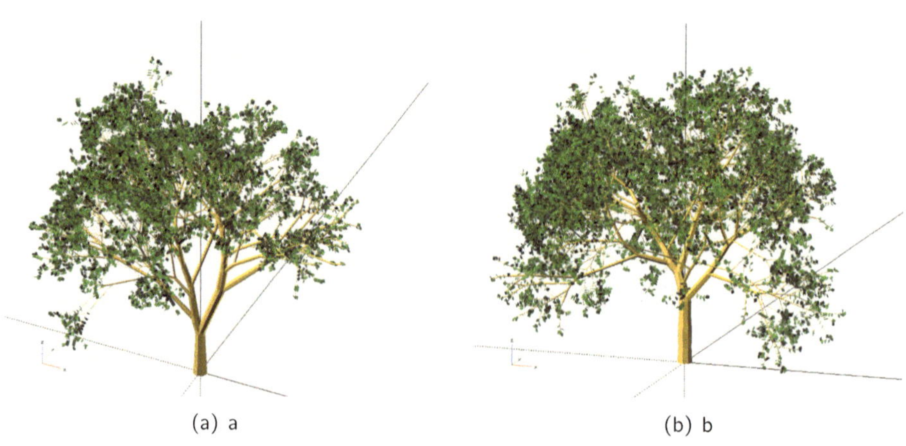

(a) a (b) b

Figure 11.5: A tree with branch angle of 40 degrees (a) and 60 degrees (b)

Project 9: Parabolic Reflector

Parabolic reflectors are fascinating. They concentrate incident parallel light or electro-magnetic radiation in a focal point. Satellite antennas or solar stoves make use of this property. In the other direction, when a light source sits in the focal point, a parabolic mirror can be used to create a parallel cone of light.

In this project we will create the geometry description for a parabolic reflector.

12.1 What's new?

We will get to know the 3D basic shape *polyhedron*. It is basically the three-dimensional counterpart of the 2D basic shape *polygon*. Creating a *polyhedron* is easy in theory, but quite challenging in practice. Therefore, we will proceed step by step and focus solely on this one novelty in this project.

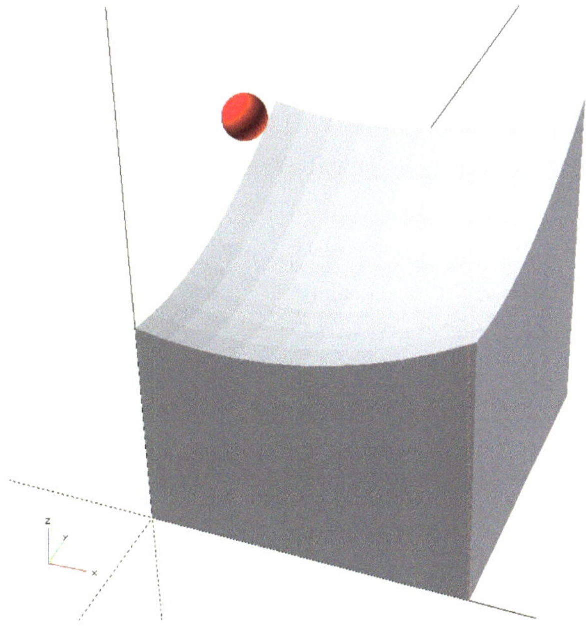

Figure 12.1: A parabolic shape

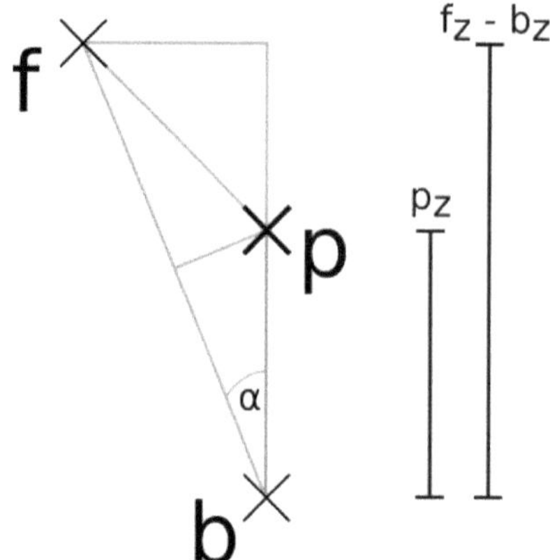

Figure 12.2: Relations between focus point f, base point b and parabola point p.

12.2   Let's go

A parabola is characterized by the fact that all points on the parabolic surface have the same distance to a reference or base surface and a focal point. Figure 12.2 shows this relation for a single point p of the parabolic surface and the corresponding points b on the base surface and f, the focus point. It can be seen that the points p, b and f form an equilateral triangle and therefore the distance between p and f and the distance between p and b are equal.

If we want to describe the geometry of a parabola, we need to determine the points p of the parabolic surface for a given focal point and a given base plane. If we look again at Figure 12.2, we see that point p lies vertically above point b. If we think of point b as part of a base surface in the X-Y plane, then we can simply take the X- and Y-coordinates of point p directly from point b. So only the Z-coordinate of p remains to be determined. Here two triangles can help us that are hidden in figure 12.2. Both triangles share the angle α. The larger of the two has its hypotenuse from f to b and the adjacent $f.z - b.z$. The smaller triangle has as its hypotenuse the length $p.z$ and as its adjacent exactly half the distance from f to b (because it is part of the equilateral triangle).

If we remember that $\cos(\alpha)$ = `adjacent / hypotenuse`, it follows for the large triangle:

```
// distance between f and b
dist_fb = norm(f - b)

cos(a) = (f.z - b.z) / dist_fb
```

For the small triangle:

```
cos(a) = (dist_fb / 2) / p.z
```

Since it is the same α in both cases, we can set the two ratios as equal and rearrange them to find the *p.z* we are looking for:

```
(f.z - b.z) / dist_fb = (dist_fb / 2) / p.z


// both sides times p.z

p.z * (f.z - b.z) / dist_fb = dist_fb / 2


// both sides divided by ((f.z - b.z) / dist_fb)

p.z = (dist_fb / 2) / ((f.z - b.z) / dist_fb)


// replace outer division by multiplication with the inverse

p.z = (dist_fb / 2) * (dist_fb / (f.z - b.z))


// multiply out: numerator times numerator, denominator times denominator

p.z = (dist_fb * dist_fb) / (2 * (f.z - b.z))
```

With that we are done! We now have a compact formula to calculate a point *p* on the parabolic surface with respect to a focus point and a base point. Let's capture this result in an OpenSCAD function *parabola_point*:

```
function parabola_point( focus_point, base_point ) =
    let ( dist_fb = norm(focus_point - base_point) )
    [
        base_point.x,
        base_point.y,
        ( dist_fb * dist_fb ) / ( 2 * (focus_point.z - base_point.z) )
    ];
```

After these preparations we can start with the definition of a module *parabola* and calculate the points on the surface of the parabola with the help of our function *parabola_point*:

```
/*
    parabola module

    - focus_point,     focus point as 3D-vector
    - base_area,       dimension of the base are as 2D-vector
    - resolution,      number of grid points as 2D-vector
*/
module parabola( focus_point, base_area, resolution = [10, 10] ){

    function parabola_point( focus_point, base_point ) =
        let ( dist_fb = norm(focus_point - base_point) )
        [
            base_point.x,
            base_point.y,
            ( dist_fb * dist_fb ) / ( 2 * (focus_point.z - base_point.z) )
        ];

    parabola_points = [
        for (
            y = [0 : base_area.y / resolution.y : base_area.y + 0.1],
            x = [0 : base_area.x / resolution.x : base_area.x + 0.1]
        )
        parabola_point( focus_point, [x,y,0] )
    ];

}

parabola(
    focus_point = [75,75,100],
    base_area   = [150,150]
);
```

Our module *parabola* has three parameters. The parameter *focus_point* sets the position of the focus point of the parabola as a three-dimensional vector. The parameter *base_ area* sets the dimension of the base surface in the form of a two-dimensional vector. Thus, we assume that our base surface is located with one corner at the origin and lies on the X-Y plane (Z = 0). The third parameter *resolution* sets the number of individual surfaces in the X- and Y-directions that the parabolic surface should consist of.

Inside the module we calculate the *parabola_ points* as an array of vectors via a generative, two-dimensional for-loop. The step size of the loop variables results from the respective number of partial surfaces (*resolution*) and the dimension of the base surface (*base_ area*). The addition of a tenth of a millimeter at the respective upper limits of the ranges serves to compensate for rounding errors. It does not mean that the parabola would become one tenth larger. Finally, inside the generative for loop, we use our function *parabola_ point* to calculate each point of the parabola surface.

Since we want to create a three-dimensional body, we still need the points of the base surface itself. We can also create these with a generative for-loop. Instead of using a function like *parabola_ point*, we can specify the three-dimensional vector of the points directly. It consists only of the X- and Y-coordinates and a constant Z-coordinate, which we set to 0:

```
module parabola( focus_point, base_area, resolution = [10, 10] ){

    /* ... */

    parabola_points = [
        for (
            y = [0 : base_area.y / resolution.y : base_area.y + 0.1],
            x = [0 : base_area.x / resolution.x : base_area.x + 0.1]
        )
        parabola_point( focus_point, [x,y,0] )
    ];

    base_points = [
        for (
            y = [0 : base_area.y / resolution.y : base_area.y + 0.1],
            x = [0 : base_area.x / resolution.x : base_area.x + 0.1]
        )
        [x, y, 0]
    ];
}
```

Now we come to a somewhat tricky part. We have to explicitly specify the individual surfaces of our geometry. Each individual surface needs four points, which have to be specified in order. This is basically like trying to trace the outer edge of the surface with a pencil all the way through without starting over. You may remember these puzzle pictures in your childhood. You were given a sheet of paper with numbered dots and then you had to connect the dots one by one to reveal the picture. We're doing something similar now.

The points in our arrays *parabola_points* and *base_points* lie one after another as a long list. Each of these lists contains (`resolution.x + 1`) * (`resolution.y + 1`) points. Thus, you can identify each point with a number. Just like the house numbers along a street. With these "house numbers" of the points we can now describe a single surface by combining four "house numbers" in a four-dimensional vector:

```
module parabola( focus_point, base_area, resolution = [10, 10] ){

    /* ... */

    size_x = resolution.x + 1;

    parabola_faces = [
        for (
            y = [0 : resolution.y - 1],
            x = [0 : resolution.x - 1]
        )
        [
            y     * size_x + x,
            y     * size_x + x + 1,
            (y+1) * size_x + x + 1,
            (y+1) * size_x + x
        ]
    ];
}
```

Since we have defined our parabola points row by row, the points in the one-dimensional array *parabola_points* lie accordingly row by row behind each other. The numbers of neighboring points in the X-direction always differ by 1. The numbers of neighboring points in the Y-direction, on the other hand, differ by `size_x = resolution.x + 1`. In other words, every *size_x* points in the array *parabola_points* a new row begins. Figure 12.3 shows this relationship schematically for a resolution of 5 x 5 surfaces. So in this example *resolution.x = 5* and correspondingly *size_x = 6*. The rows thus start at 0, 6, 12, etc.

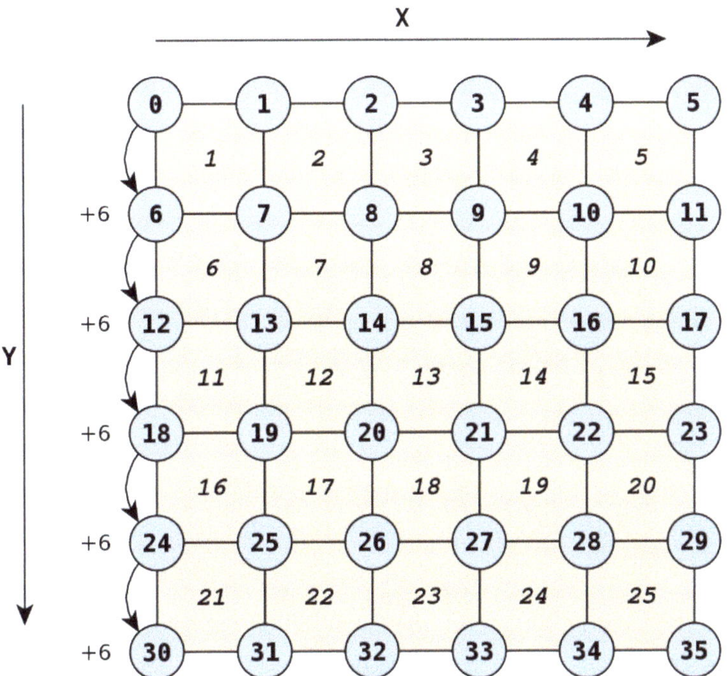

Figure 12.3: Numbering of points and associated areas at a resolution of 5 x 5

So if we want to find the number of the first point of a surface, we first have to calculate the start number of the row (y * size_x) and then add the X-position of the point (+ x). The next point of the surface is right next to it. So you only have to add 1 to the previous number (y * size_x + x + 1). The third point is one row lower (y + 1). Therefore its number is (y + 1) * size_x + x + 1. The fourth point is in the same row before the third point. So we have to subtract 1 again from the number of the third point ((y + 1) * size_x + x). If we repeat this for all surfaces, we get the desired list of *parabola_surfaces*.

For the surfaces of the base we can proceed in a similar way:

```
module parabola( focus_point, base_area, resolution = [10, 10] ){

    /* ... */

    size_x = resolution.x + 1;

    /* ... */
```

```
    size_ppoints = len( parabola_points );

    base_faces = [
        for (
            y = [0 : resolution.y - 1],
            x = [0 : resolution.x - 1]
        )
        [ y     * size_x + x     + size_ppoints,
          y     * size_x + x + 1 + size_ppoints,
         (y+1) * size_x + x + 1 + size_ppoints,
         (y+1) * size_x + x     + size_ppoints]
    ];
}
```

Since we will later append the *base_ points* to the *parabola_ points*, the numbers of the base points will shift by the number of parabola points. This shift is achieved by adding *size_ ppoints*. Otherwise, nothing changes in the determination of the surfaces.

We have now defined the surfaces of the parabola and the base. What is still missing are the surfaces of the sides. Let's start with one side:

```
module parabola( focus_point, base_area, resolution = [10, 10] ){

    /* ... */

    size_x = resolution.x + 1;

    /* ... */

    size_ppoints = len( parabola_points );

    /* ... */

    side_faces_1 = [
        for ( x = [0 : resolution.x - 1] )
        [ x,
          x + 1,
          x + 1 + size_ppoints,
          x     + size_ppoints ]
    ];
}
```

For the first side we run only once along the X-direction and connect the points from the array *parabola_points* with their corresponding points from the array *base_points* in pairs. Since the numbers of the *base_points* start at *size_ppoints*, we find the corresponding additions at points 3 and 4 of the surface.

The opposite side can be described in a similar way. Here we need to shift the numbers so that we do not run along the first row, but along the last row:

```
module parabola( focus_point, base_area, resolution = [10, 10] ){

    /* ... */

    size_x = resolution.x + 1;

    /* ... */

    size_ppoints = len( parabola_points );

    /* ... */

    last_row = resolution.y * size_x;

    side_faces_2 = [
        for ( x = [0 : resolution.x - 1] )
        [
            last_row + x,
            last_row + x + 1,
            last_row + x + 1 + size_ppoints,
            last_row + x     + size_ppoints
        ]
    ];
}
```

We achieve this by calculating the starting number of the last row (`last_row = resolution.y * size_x;`) and adding it at each point of the surface. Otherwise, everything remains the same as for side surface 1.

Now we come to the other two side faces. For these we do not have to run along the outer rows, but along the outer columns:

```
module parabola( focus_point, base_area, resolution = [10, 10] ){

    /* ... */

    size_x = resolution.x + 1;
```

```
    /* ... */

    size_ppoints = len( parabola_points );

    /* ... */

    side_faces_3 = [
        for ( y = [0 : resolution.y - 1] )
        [
             y        * size_x,
            (y + 1) * size_x,
            (y + 1) * size_x + size_ppoints,
             y        * size_x + size_ppoints
        ]
    ];

    last_col = resolution.x;

    side_faces_4 = [
        for ( y = [0 : resolution.y - 1] )
        [
            last_col +  y        * size_x,
            last_col + (y + 1) * size_x,
            last_col + (y + 1) * size_x + size_ppoints,
            last_col +  y        * size_x + size_ppoints
        ]
    ];
}
```

Overall, we see the same scheme for side faces 3 and 4 as for side faces 1 and 2. Side face 4 differs from side face 3 only in that we have shifted the numbers by the starting number of the last column. While the numbers of the points along the X-direction have the distance 1, the numbers of the points along the Y-direction have the distance *size_x*.

Grokking the logic of the numbering of the points is not easy, especially in the beginning. It helps a lot to sketch the geometry on a sheet of paper and to label it with the numbers of the points. Just as it can be seen in figure 12.3.

Now we have finally gathered enough information to create our geometry with the basic shape *polyhedron*:

```
module parabola( focus_point, base_area, resolution = [10, 10] ){

    /* ... */
```

```
    polyhedron(
        points = concat( parabola_points, base_points ),
        faces  = concat( parabola_faces,
                         base_faces,
                         side_faces_1,
                         side_faces_2,
                         side_faces_3,
                         side_faces_4)
    );
}
```

We use the *concat* function to concatenate our point and surface sets and pass them as parameters *points* and *faces* to the 3D base shape *polyhedron*. If we now run a preview (*F5*) we should finally be able to see our parabola.

There are certainly use cases where you don't want the full body below the parabola. We can adjust our module *parabola* in one place to provide the possibility to create only the parabola surface itself with a given thickness:

```
module parabola(
    focus_point,
    base_area,
    resolution = [10, 10],
    thickness  = 0
){

    /* ... */

    base_points = [
        for (
            y = [0 : base_area.y / resolution.y : base_area.y + 0.1],
            x = [0 : base_area.x / resolution.x : base_area.x + 0.1]
        )
        let ( p = parabola_point( focus_point, [x,y,0] ) )
        if (thickness > 0)
            [x, y, p.z - thickness]
        else
            [x, y, 0]
    ];

    /* ... */

}
```

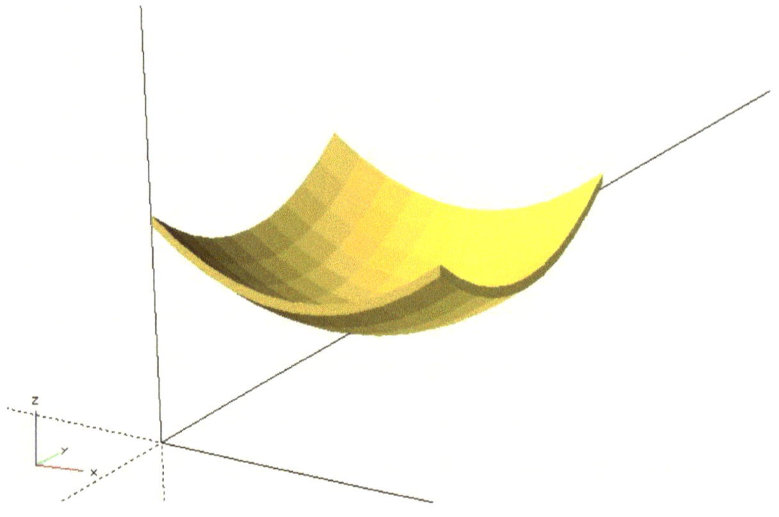

Figure 12.4: Parabolic shape without substructure

For this extension we give our module *parabola* another parameter *thickness*, which gets the default value 0. Inside the module we change the calculation of the base points slightly. By means of *let* we calculate the current parabola point again and keep it in the variable *p*. Subsequently, we carry out a case distinction. If the parameter *thickness* is greater than zero, then we create a base point that is exactly *thickness* away from the parabola point *p*. Otherwise, if *thickness* is equal to 0, we create the base point as usual on the X-Y plane.

With this change, we can now create pure parabolic surfaces without a substructure (Figure 12.4).

The basic 3D shape *polyhedron* is certainly not the first choice when you want to describe a 3D geometry with OpenSCAD. Using *polyhedron* requires some planning and is not free of subtle problems. For example, surfaces may not be displayed correctly. This generally has two possible causes. If the display errors only occur in the preview (*F5*), but not in the actual render (*F6*), then increasing the *convexity* parameter of the basic 3D shape *polyhedron* can help. By default this parameter has the value 1.

The second cause of errors is a bit more troublesome to fix. This is because the surfaces you have defined are only visible from one direction. If you would look from the inside of the object to the outside, you could see through the surfaces. Which side of the surfaces is visible and which is not depends on the order of the points with which we build up a surface. So a surface with the points [0, 1, 2, 3] or the points [3, 2, 1, 0] differs in whether the front or the back side is visible. A good tool to deal with such problems is to define a function *flip* which flips the order of the elements in a four-dimensional vector:

```
function flip(vec) = [ vec[3], vec[2], vec[1], vec[0] ];
```

If the rendering of a set of surfaces is not OK, one can bring the function *flip* to bear on the definition of the surfaces and see if this solves the problem. This would look like this, for example:

```
side_faces_1 = [
    for ( x = [0 : resolution.x - 1] )
    flip ([
        x,
        x + 1,
        x + 1 + size_ppoints,
        x     + size_ppoints
    ])
];
```

All in all, you will probably use *polyhedron* rather rarely. However, it represents a powerful tool with which one can solve difficult modeling tasks.

12.3   3D printing tips

The further the focal point is away from the parabolic surface, the flatter the surface will become. In such a case, try to print the parabolic surface vertically. This will make the surface of the parabola finer, as 3D printers usually have a higher resolution in the X-Y plane than in the Z-axis.

If you need a parabola with a different outer shape, e.g. round, you can easily achieve such a shape by using the Boolean operation *intersection* with, e.g., a cylinder.

Project 10: Fan Wheel

In this project we want to construct a parameterizable fan wheel, in which the angle of attack and the torsion of the blades are adjustable in particular.

13.1 What's new?

We will learn about a new property of the *linear_extrude* transformation and use the mathematical functions *abs* and *atan*.

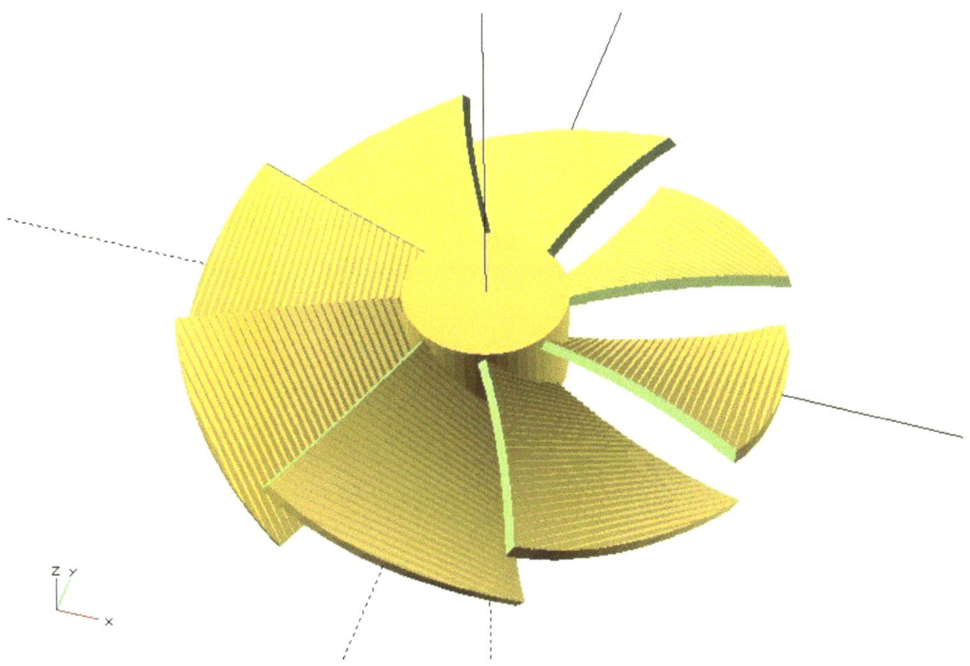

Figure 13.1: A parameterizable fan wheel

13.2 Let's go

Let's start with the definition of a module *fan_wheel*, a set of parameters and a submodule *blade*, where we will describe the geometry of a single blade of the fan wheel:

```
module fan_wheel(
    outer_radius    = 55,
    inner_radius    = 15,
    blade_count     = 8,
    outer_width     = 50,
    inner_width     = 20,
    thickness       = 2,
    twist           = -30,
    angle_of_attack = 45,
){

    module blade() {

    }

    blade(); // debug
}

fan_wheel();
```

Except for the parameter *blade_count*, which sets the number of fan blades, all other parameters refer to geometrical properties of a single blade. Figure 13.2 shows schematically which properties of a blade are referred to by the parameters *outer_radius*, *inner_radius*, *outer_width* and *inner_width*. We will derive the values *inner_height* and *blade_height* in figure 13.2 later. The parameters *twist* and *angle_of_attack* affect the twist of the fan blade and the angle of the blade at the fan hub. The parameter *thickness* sets the thickness of the fan blade.

Inside the module *fan_wheel* we have created the submodule *blade* as well as a test instance of this submodule. Let's start with the geometry description of a single blade:

```
module fan_wheel(
    /* ... */
){

    module blade() {
```

```
        inner_height =
            cos(
                asin( inner_width / ( 2 * inner_radius ) )
            ) * inner_radius;

        blade_height = outer_radius - inner_height;

        translate( [0, inner_height, 0] )
        rotate( [-90, 0, 0] )
        linear_extrude(
            height    = blade_height,
            twist     = twist,
            slices    = 10 ,
            convexity = 10
        )
        square( [outer_width, thickness], center = true );
    }

    blade(); // debug
}
```

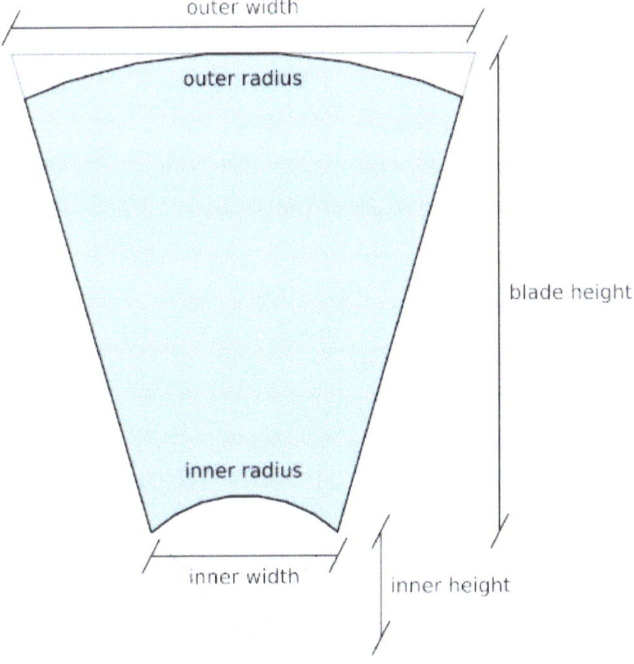

Figure 13.2: Dimensions of a blade

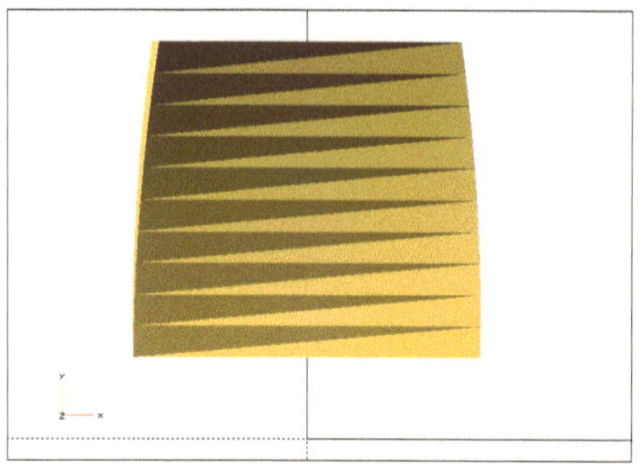

Figure 13.3: Extruded and twisted rectangle

We first calculate the values *inner_height* and *blade_height* (Figure 13.2). The *inner_height* is the point where the vertical with distance `inner_width / 2` from the origin and the circle with *inner_radius* meet. To calculate the *inner_height* we need the angle between the radius and the vertical at this intersection (`asin( inner_width / ( 2 * inner_radius )`). Then we can determine the *inner_height* using the cosine and the *inner_radius*. The *blade_height* is the remainder of the distance from *inner_height* to *outer_radius*.

We model the blade itself using the 2D basic shape *square* and a linear extrusion. We use the *twist* parameter of *linear_extrude* to rotate the basic shape during extrusion (Figure <imgref>). The parameter *slices* can be used to set how many subdivisions *linear_extrude* should make along the extrusion to model the twist. The parameter *convexity* is an auxiliary parameter that ensures that the preview of the geometry is calculated cleanly and has no holes. By default, this parameter has a value of 1. If you find errors in the geometry during preview, it is worth trying to increase this parameter. A value of 10 should be sufficient in practically all cases.

Now we will describe the tapered shape of the fan blade using a Boolean difference operation:

```
module fan_wheel( /* ... */ ) {

    module blade() {

        /* ... */
```

```
    angle =
        atan(
            ( ( outer_width / 2 * cos( abs( twist ) ) ) -
              ( inner_width / 2 )
            ) / blade_height
        );

    height = sin( abs( twist ) ) * outer_width / 2 +
            thickness;

    width = outer_width / 2 - inner_width / 2;

    depth  =
        sqrt(
            pow( ( outer_width / 2 * cos( abs( twist ) ) ) -
                ( inner_width / 2 ), 2 ) +
            pow( blade_height, 2 )
        ) + thickness;

    difference(){
        translate( [0, inner_height, 0] )
        rotate( [-90, 0, 0] )
        linear_extrude(
            height    = blade_height,
            twist     = twist,
            slices    = 10 ,
            convexity = 10
        )
        square( [outer_width, thickness], center = true );

        for (i = [0 : 1])
        mirror( [i, 0, 0] )
        translate([
            inner_width / 2,
            inner_height,
            -height
        ])
        rotate( [0, 0, -angle] )
        translate( [0, -depth / 2, 0] )
        cube( [width * 2, depth * 1.5, 2 * height] );
    }
}

blade(); // debug
}
```

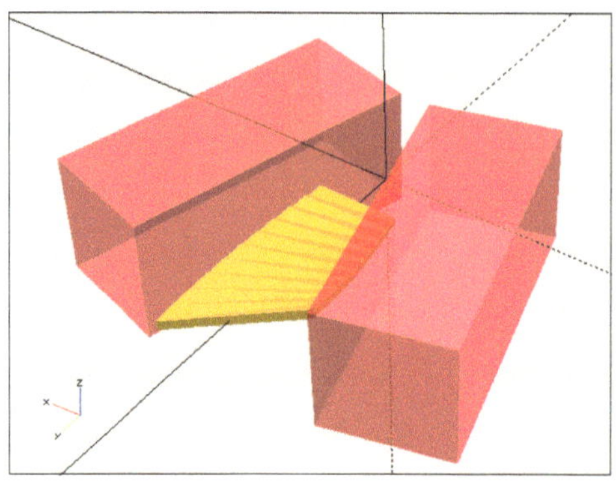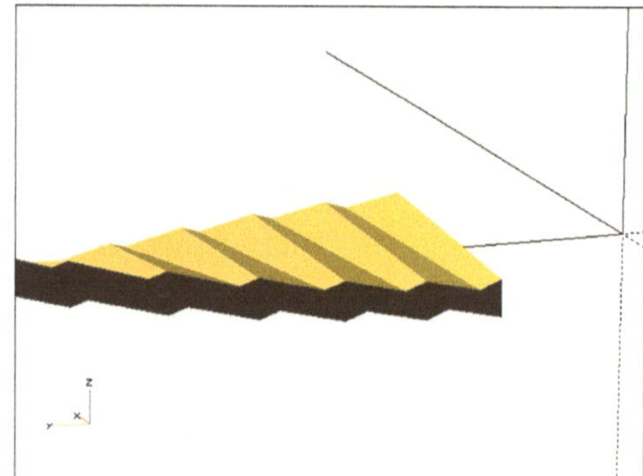

Figure 13.4: Cutting off the side parts using Boolean difference results in jagged edges

We first calculate the angle of the side via the arc tangent function *atan*. It gets as parameter the difference between *inner_width* and the *outer_width* rotated by *twist*. We use the absolute value (*abs*) of *twist* in this case to get the same result even with a negative twist parameter. Afterwards we determine the minimal *height*, *width* and *depth* of the box (*cube*) that we want to subtract from the fan blade.

After these preparations, we can now move our fan blade description into the geometry set of a Boolean difference operation and define two boxes that we subtract from the fan blade. Since the sides are mirror symmetric, we can create the two boxes using a combination of for-loop and mirror transformation. We make the box that will be subtracted slightly larger than generally necessary. This way, we also cover situations that may arise due to an "extreme" parameterization of the fan wheel (for example, when the *outer_width* is very small). Figure 13.4 shows the position of the described boxes. It also shows that now the sides of our fan blade have become jagged. This jagged structure comes from the fact that the basic 2D shape of our blade is a very thin rectangle, which is internally formed by only two triangles. These are now no longer sufficient to cleanly describe the slanted side edges of the fan blade.

We can fix this problem by using a polygon as 2D base shape instead of a simple rectangle. We need to design the polygon in such a way that it has enough internal "resolution". To do this, we need to use a little trick:

```
module fan_wheel( /* ... */ ) {

    module blade() {

        /* ... */

        blade_divisions = 10;

        difference() {

            translate( [0, inner_height, 0] )
            rotate( [-90, 0, 0] )
            linear_extrude(
                height    = blade_height,
                twist     = twist,
                slices    = 10 ,
                convexity = 10
            )
            translate([
                -outer_width / 2,
                -thickness / 2
            ])
            polygon( concat(
                [for (i = [0 : blade_divisions])
                    [i * outer_width / blade_divisions, (i % 2) * 0.0001]
                ],
                [for (i = [blade_divisions : -1 : 0])
                    [i * outer_width / blade_divisions,
                     thickness + (i % 2) * 0.0001]
                ]
            ));

            /* ... */

        } // difference
    }

    blade(); // debug
}
```

We create the polygon from two concatenated (*concat*) arrays. The first array describes
the points of the polygon in X-direction at height 0. The second array describes the points
of the polygon in opposite X-direction at height *thickness*. If all our points in forward
and backward direction **exactly** lie on a line, then OpenSCAD will optimize these points

Figure 13.5: Repairing the jagged edges using polygon

away. To prevent this from happening, we need to move every other point minimally in the Y-direction. We use the modulo operation for this purpose. The expression `i % 2` alternates between 0 and 1 for consecutive *i*. Our Y-coordinate therefore jumps back and forth from point to point between 0 and 0.0001. By doing this, we prevent OpenSCAD from optimizing and achieve the desired goal of a higher geometric resolution of our 2D base shape. Figure 13.5 shows how this eliminates the jagged sides of the fan blade.

Our fan blade is now almost finished. We only have to rotate it by its *angle_of_attack* and add the outer and inner radius to the geometry description. For the outer radius we can do this with a Boolean intersection and for the inner radius we can use another Boolean difference:

```
module fan_wheel(
    /* ... */
){

    module blade() {

        /* ... */

        difference(){

            intersection(){

                rotate( [0, -angle_of_attack, 0] )
                difference() {

                    /* ... */

                }
```

```
            // outer radius
            translate( [0, 0, -height] )
            cylinder(
                r = outer_radius,
                h = 2 * height,
                $fn = 100
            );

        }

        // inner radius
        translate( [0, 0, -height] )
        cylinder( r = inner_radius, h = 2 * height, $fn = 50);
        }
    }

    blade(); // debug
}
```

We apply the intersection and difference operation only after the rotation by *angle_of_attack* so that the outer and inner edges of the fan blade remain vertical regardless of the rotation. This completely describes our submodule *blade* (Figure 13.6).

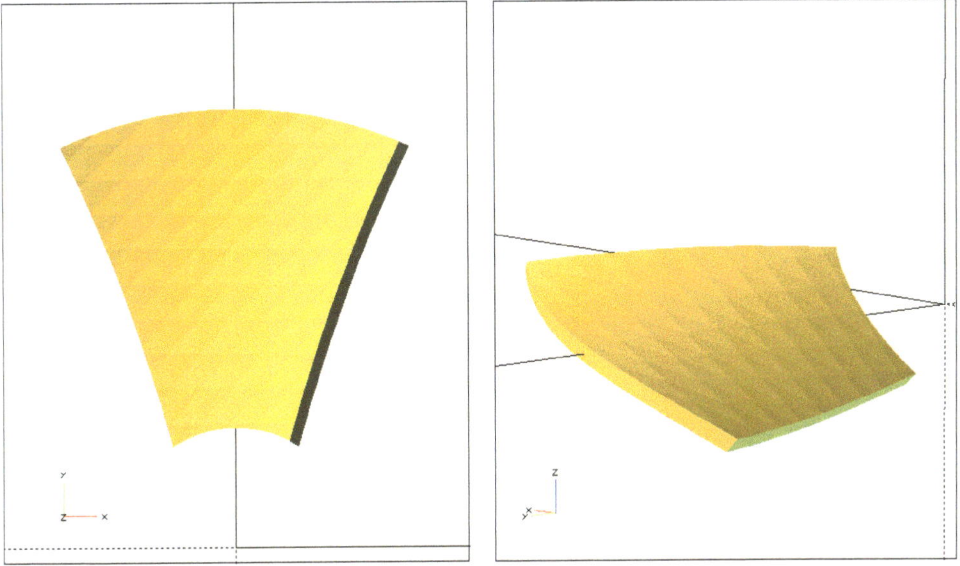

Figure 13.6: Finished fan blade viewed from above and in perspective

The completion of the main module is now relatively straightforward:

```
module fan_wheel(
    /* ... */
){

    module blade() {

    }

    // hub
    hub_height =
        sin( abs( angle_of_attack ) ) * inner_width / 2 +
        thickness;

    translate( [0, 0, -hub_height] )
    cylinder( r = inner_radius, h = hub_height * 2, $fn = 50);

    // blades
    for(i = [0 : 360 / blade_count : 359])
    rotate( [0, 0, i] )
    blade();

}
```

We first determine the height of our hub (*hub_height*) depending on the angle of attack, the inner width and the material thickness. Then we create the hub as a simple cylinder and center this cylinder along the Z-axis. We now describe the blades using a for-loop, where the step size of the loop variable *i* results from the parameterized number of blades (`360 / blade_count`). We use the loop variable *i* to distribute our submodule *blade* with an appropriate number of copies over 360 degrees by means of rotation around the Z axis (`rotate( [0, 0, i] )`).

With this our fan wheel is finished (Figure 13.7)!

13.3   3D printing tips

The blades of the fan wheel have a strong overhang, especially towards the outside. Here it is recommended to print with a low layer height and a larger line width. If your 3D printer has a 0.4mm print nozzle, you can print lines with a width of 0.5mm to 0.6mm

Figure 13.7: Differently parameterized variants of the fan wheel

without problems. As layer thickness you can go down to 0.075mm with most printers. Another trick is to slow down the print speed for the outer walls of the print. This allows the filament to cool down more as it is exposed to the print head blower for longer.

If you print the fan wheel with support structures, you should activate the option for forming a *support roof*. This will make the interface between the support structure and the 3D model cleaner. An alternative to using support structures is to split the fan wheel into an upper and a lower half using a Boolean intersection:

```
// upper half
intersection() {
    fan_wheel();

    translate([-100,-100,0])
    cube([200,200,100]);
}

// lower half
translate([120,0,0])
rotate([180,0,0])
intersection() {
    fan_wheel();

    translate([-100,-100,-100])
    cube([200,200,100]);
}
```

After printing both halves, they can then be glued together. This can be done, for example, with superglue and activator, or with a two-component adhesive. To ensure a clean alignment of the two halves, it can be helpful to drill two holes in the hub using a Boolean difference operation and to insert two pins in these holes and use them as alignment aids when gluing.

What is missing ?

In the past 10 projects we got to know almost the entire range of functions in OpenSCAD. Figures 14.1, 14.2 and 14.3 provide an overview of this. In the following we will briefly discuss the functions that we have left out so far.

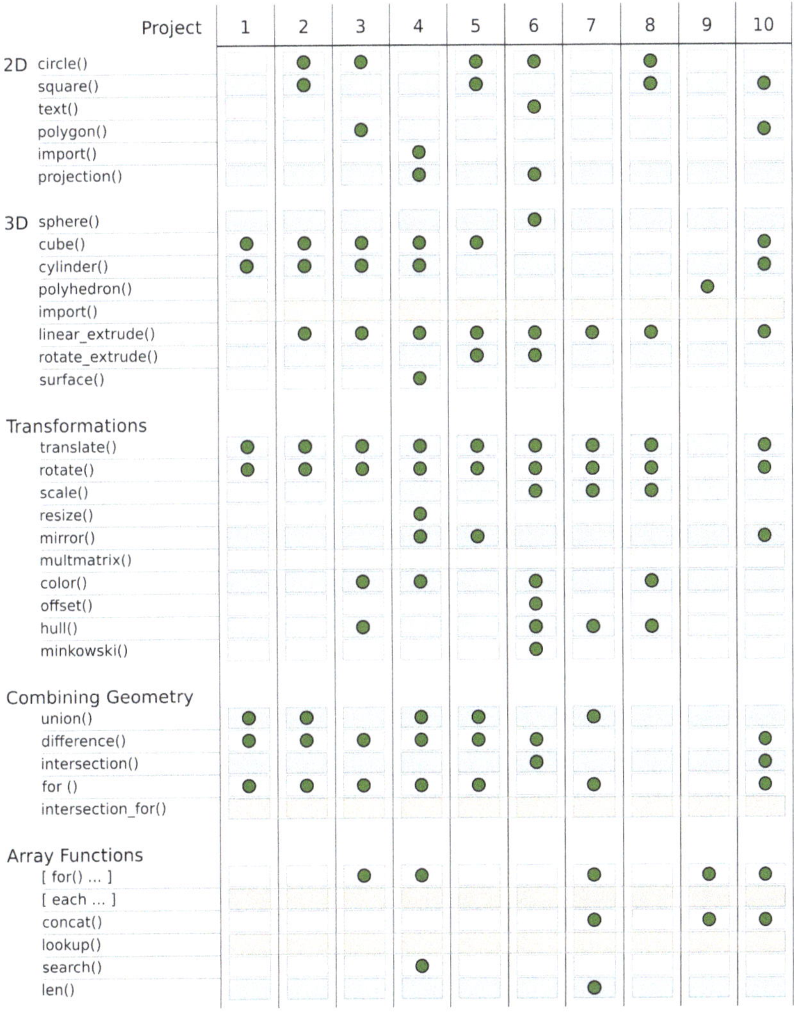

Project	1	2	3	4	5	6	7	8	9	10
2D circle()		●	●		●	●		●		
square()		●			●			●		●
text()						●				
polygon()			●							●
import()				●						
projection()				●		●				
3D sphere()						●				
cube()	●	●	●	●	●					●
cylinder()	●	●	●	●						●
polyhedron()									●	
import()										
linear_extrude()		●	●	●	●	●	●	●		●
rotate_extrude()					●	●				
surface()				●						
Transformations translate()	●	●	●	●	●	●	●	●		●
rotate()	●	●	●	●	●	●	●	●		●
scale()						●	●	●		
resize()				●						
mirror()				●	●					●
multmatrix()										
color()			●	●		●		●		
offset()						●				
hull()			●			●	●	●		
minkowski()						●				
Combining Geometry union()	●	●		●	●		●			
difference()	●	●	●	●	●	●				●
intersection()						●				●
for ()	●	●	●	●	●		●			●
intersection_for()										
Array Functions [for() ...]			●	●			●		●	●
[each ...]										
concat()							●		●	●
lookup()										
search()				●						
len()							●			

Figure 14.1: Overview of the functions used in the projects. Part 1 from 3

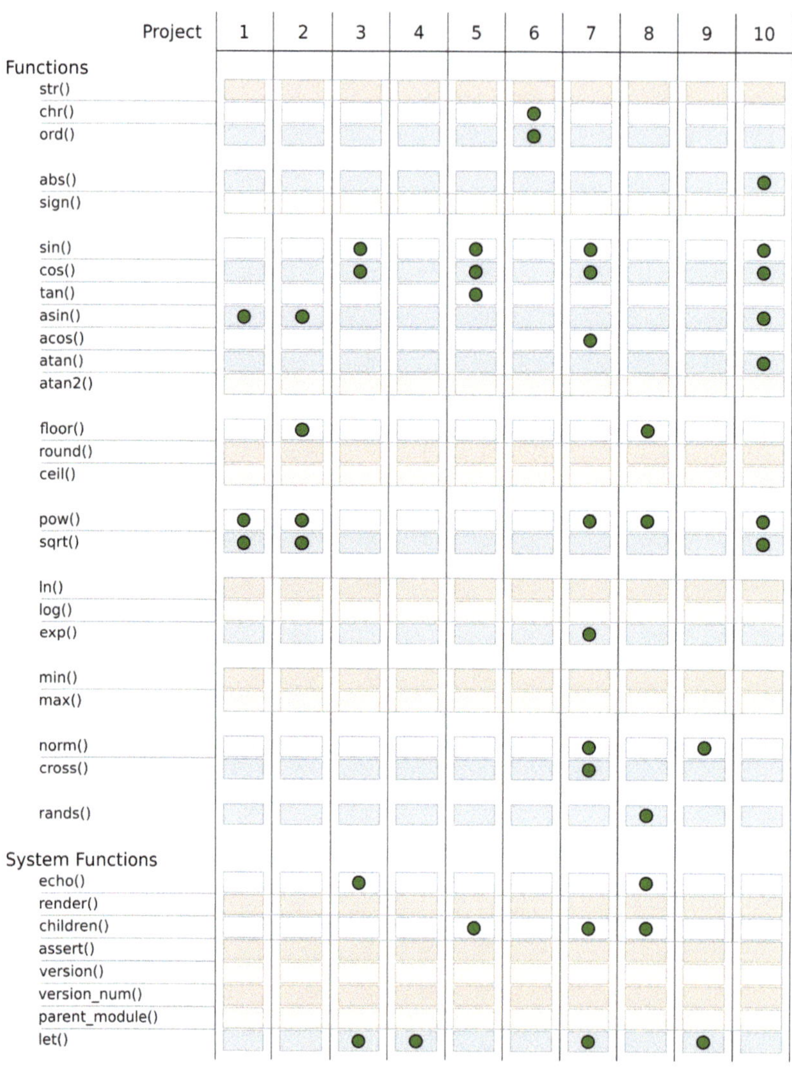

Figure 14.2: Overview of the functions used in the projects. Part 2 from 3

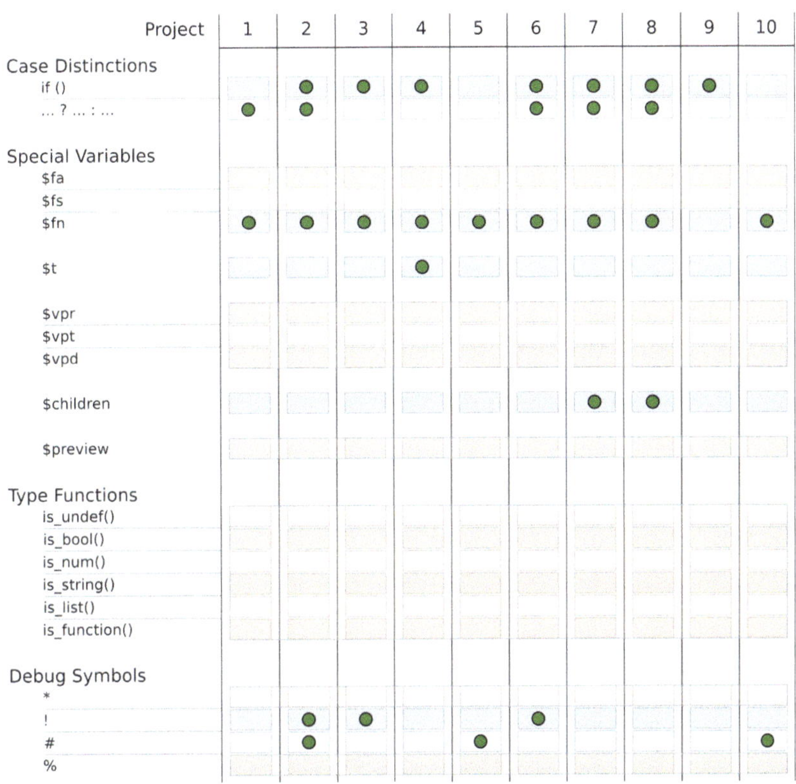

Project	1	2	3	4	5	6	7	8	9	10
Case Distinctions										
if ()		●	●	●		●	●	●	●	
... ? ... : ...	●	●				●	●	●		
Special Variables										
$fa										
$fs										
$fn	●	●	●	●	●	●	●	●		●
$t				●						
$vpr										
$vpt										
$vpd										
$children							●	●		
$preview										
Type Functions										
is_undef()										
is_bool()										
is_num()										
is_string()										
is_list()										
is_function()										
Debug Symbols										
*										
!		●	●			●				
#		●			●					●
%										

Figure 14.3: Overview of the functions used in the projects. Part 3 from 3

14.1 Geometry Functions

In project 4, we used the *import* function to import .svg files as a 2D basic shape. However, the *import* function can also import 3D data in .stl, .off, .amf and .3mf formats. Especially if you want to use a complex and computationally intensive OpenSCAD geometry in another project, using *import* instead of *include* or *use* can be useful. This way you avoid in many cases a recalculation of the complex geometry. The disadvantage is, of course, that you can no longer parameterize the imported geometry directly.

The only transformation we have not used is the *multmatrix* transformation. It allows to perform an *affine transformation* of the geometry via a transformation matrix. The matrix is a 4 x 3 or 4 x 4 matrix whose cells have the following meaning:

```
M = [
    // the first row is concerned with X
    [
        1, // scaling in X-direction
        0, // shear of X along Y
        0, // shear of X along Z
        0, // translation along X
    ],

    // the second row is concerned with Y
    [
        0, // shear of Y along X
        1, // scaling in Y-direction
        0, // shear of Y along Z
        0, // translation along Y
    ],

    // the third row is concerned with Z
    [
        0, // shear of Z along X
        0, // shear of Z along Y
        0, // scaling in Z-direction
        0, // translation along Z
    ],

    // the fourth row is always:
    [0, 0, 0, 1]

];

multmatrix(M)
cube([10,10,10]);
```

Since the fourth row of the matrix M is fixed, it can also be omitted when using *multmatrix*. With the appropriate assignment of the entries of matrix M one can perform any translations or rotations and combine them by matrix multiplication. In practice, *multmatrix* is rarely used. Only the possibility to shear an object in a certain direction is sometimes useful.

We have used for-loops in many places in the 10 projects. The resulting geometries are implicitly combined as a Boolean union. This can be seen well in the following example:

```
module test() {

    echo($children);

    children();
}

test() {
    sphere(5);

    translate( [10, 0, 0] )
    sphere(5);

    translate( [20, 0, 0] )
    sphere(5);
}

test()
for(i = [0:2])
translate( [10 * i, 10, 0] )
sphere(5);
```

We define a module *test*, which outputs the number of elements of the subsequent geometry in the console window. If we use *test* with a geometry set ({ ... }) we get an output of 3 in the above example. If we use *test* with a for-loop, we get an output of 1. Thus, the geometries defined by the for-loop are combined into a single geometry. This means that it is not possible to describe a set of geometries with a for-loop and then apply the Boolean operation *intersection* on this set of geometries. Exactly for this case there is the *intersection_ for*-loop in OpenSCAD. In practice, this type of for-loop is rarely used. But it can be used to create interesting geometries. This diamond-like geometry may serve as an example:

```
M = [
    [1,0,1,0],
    [0,1,0,0],
    [0,0,1,0]
];

intersection_for(i = [0:60:359])
rotate( [0, 0, i] )
multmatrix( M )
cube( 10, center = true );
```

14.2   Array Methods

We have used generative for-loops in many places to define arrays. Within such a generative for-loop, the keyword *each* can be used to "unpack" a vector. Let's look at the following example:

```
vectors = [
    [1,2,3],
    [4,5,6],
    [7,8,9]
];

flattened = [ for (v = vectors) each v];

echo( flattened );
```

The variable *flattened* is a one-dimensional array, which contains all entries of the two-dimensional array *vectors*. The console output for *flattened* therefore results in ECHO: [1, 2, 3, 4, 5, 6, 7, 8, 9].

The *lookup* function interpolates values in an array of number pairs to be linearly. An example:

```
values = [
    [-3,  2],
    [ 0, 10],
    [ 1, 50],
    [ 4,  0]
];

echo( lookup(-1,   values) );
echo( lookup( 0,   values) );
echo( lookup( 0.5, values) );
echo( lookup( 3,   values) );
```

The console output for this looks like this:

```
ECHO: 7.33333
ECHO: 10
ECHO: 30
ECHO: 16.6667
```

The *lookup* function searches the array of number pairs passed to it for the two adjacent number pairs whose first values span an interval in which the passed search parameter lies. Subsequently, the second values of these two pairs are averaged such that the resulting average corresponds to the proximity of the search parameter to the respective first values.

14.3 Functions

We have used a large part of the functions provided by OpenSCAD in our projects. We did not use the functions *str, sign, atan2, round, ceil, ln, log, min* and *max*.

The function *str* creates a single, contiguous string from its parameters. You remember the variable **srnd** from project 8? We used the variable for initializing random numbers and output its value to the console using **echo(srnd);** to remember it for later, manual use. We could have made this console output a bit more readable with the *str* function, e.g. **echo(str("As initialization value ", srnd, " was used."));**.

The function *sign* returns the sign of a number. For negative numbers *sign* returns a –1, for positive numbers a 1 and for zero a 0.

The function *atan2* is a variant of the arc tangent. The "normal" arc tangent cannot distinguish between y/x and –y/–x, since the minus signs would cancel out in the second case. The function *atan2* solves this problem by passing y and x as separate parameters to the function.

The *round* function rounds the passed decimal value commercially. The function *ceil* always rounds up the passed value.

The function *ln* returns the natural logarithm of the given number. The function *log* returns the logarithm to the base 10.

The function *min* returns as result the smallest value of the parameters passed to it. If the parameter consists of only one vector, the smallest element within the vector is returned. The function *max* behaves analogously. It returns the largest element in each case.

14.4   System Methods

In rare cases it can happen that the preview (*F5*) of a geometry fails and artifacts occur which cannot be dealt with by other means (e.g. a *convexity* parameter). With the function *render*, which can be prepended to any geometry like a transformation (e.g. `render() sphere( 10 );`), one can force OpenSCAD to calculate the corresponding part of the geometry completely even during a preview.

Another use of *render* is to convert complex geometry into a 3D model already in the preview, thus making the preview smoother. This can be particularly helpful for complex Boolean operations.

The *assert* function facilitates checking of assumptions and allows to output an appropriate error message if these assumptions are not met. This is especially useful when we develop modules that are to be used by others as a library. Let's assume we expect a three-dimensional vector as input. Then a check could look like this:

```
module my_module( size ) {

    assert(
        len(size) == 3,
        "Parameter size must be a three-dimensional vector!"
    );
}
```

If we would now call the module e.g. with a simple number, we would get an error message in the console:

```
ERROR: Assertion '(len(size) == 3)' failed: "Parameter size must be a
three-dimensional vector!"
```

The type checking functions described below can be very useful in this context.

The functions *version* and *version_num* return the current version of OpenSCAD. The *version* function returns a three-dimensional vector with the individual version components. The function *version_num* returns a single number uniquely representing the respective version.

Such a version query is useful when we develop a geometry library and use functions that are not available in earlier versions of OpenSCAD or have been parameterized differently. By appropriate case distinctions one can achieve it that the library remains stable over several versions of OpenSCAD.

The function *parent_module* returns the name of a parent module within a module hierarchy, if all modules within the hierarchy access child elements by means of *children*. The official manual of OpenSCAD gives the generation of a material list as an application example. In practice, this function does not play any role.

14.5   Special Variables

In our projects we often used the special variable *$fn* to set the level of detail of curved geometries. In a similar way, the level of detail of curved geometries can also be controlled using the variables *$fa* and *$fs*. With *$fa* you can set the minimum angles of a geometry and with *$fs* the minimum size of the individual surfaces. In both cases, smaller values result in a finer geometry. By default *$fa* is set to 12 and *$fs* to 2.

The special variables *$vpr*, *$vpt* and *$vpd* provide information about the current perspective in the output window when a new preview is rendered. *$vpr* provides the rotation, *$vpt* the displacement and *$vpd* the distance of the camera.

By setting these variables you can change the perspective in the output window. This could be used, for example, to create tracking shots in connection with the animation capabilities of OpenSCAD.

The special variable *$preview* returns **true** if a preview (*F5*) is run and **false** if a full geometry render (*F6*) is performed.

14.6   Type Checking Functions

OpenSCAD provides a number of functions that can be used to check the type of a variable. This check is especially useful in connection with the *assert* function, or in case you want to provide a parameter with double functionality. An existing example of this is the *scale* parameter of the *linear_ extrude* transformation. The parameter can be either a number or a vector. If it is a number, the underlying 2D shape is scaled equally in all directions. If the parameter is a vector, individual scaling can be specified for the X- and Y-directions.

The available type functions are: *is_ undef, is_ bool, is_ num, is_ string, is_ list* and (in future OpenSCAD versions) *is_ function*. With *list* any kind of arrays or vectors are meant.

14.7   Debug Symbols

Besides the known debug characters ! and # there is also the * character and the % character. With the * character you can "disable" a geometry part. It is an alternative to commenting it out. With the % character you can make a geometry part transparent.

With this final short summary you now know **all** OpenSCAD functions!

Quick Reference

Finally, here is a compact quick reference of the most important OpenSCAD functions and their parameters.

15.1   2D Geometry

15.1.1   Circle

```
circle(
    r,        // radius
    d         // or diameter
);
```

15.1.2   Rectangle

```
square(
    size,        // a single value creates a square,
                 // a two-dimensional vector a rectangle

    center       // if true, the rectangle is centered over the origin
);
```

15.1.3   Polygon

```
polygon(
    points,      // array of two-dimensional vectors as set of points

    paths,       // optional array with point indices if the polygon has also
                 // inner "negative" paths

    convexity    // Optimization parameters for preview. If you experience
                 // rendering errors in preview, increase this value. A value
                 // of 10 should work in most cases.
);
```

15.1.4   Text

```
text(
    text,       // the text as string

    size,       // the height of a standard uppercase letter

    font,       // the font name as string (project 6)

    halign,     // horizontal alignment given as string
                // possible values: "left", "center", "right"

    valign,     // vertical alignment given as string
                // possible values: "top", "center", "baseline", "bottom"

    spacing,    // adjustment factor to influence spacing between letters

    direction,  // writing direction, possible values:
                // "ltr" -> from left to right
                // "rtl" -> from right to left
                // "ttb" -> from top to bottom
                // "btt" -> from bottom to top

    language,   // language given as short string. "en", "de", ...

    script      // lettering system, default value is "latin"
);
```

15.1.5   Import of Geometries

```
import(
    file,       // filename of a `.svg`- or `.dxf`-file

    convexity   // Optimization parameters for preview. If you experience
                // rendering errors in preview, increase this value. A value
                // of 10 should work in most cases.

    layer       // layer name in case of a `.dxf`-file
);
```

15.1.6 Projection

```
projection(
    cut       // if "true", the subsequent geometry is cut in the X-Y-Plane
              // instead of being projected onto it
);
```

15.2 3D Geometry

15.2.1 Sphere

```
sphere(
    r,       // radius
    d        // or diameter
);
```

15.2.2 Box

```
cube(
    size,      // a single value results in a cube
               // a three-dimensional vector results in a cuboid a.k.a. box

    center     // if "true", the box is centered around the origin
);
```

15.2.3 Cylinder

```
cylinder(
    h,            // height of the cylinder

    r,            // radius, or alternatively
    r1,           // lower radius and
    r2,           // upper radius

    d,            // diameter, or alternatively
    d1,           // lower diameter and
    d2,           // upper diameter
```

```
        center        // if "true", the cylinder is centered along the Z-Axis
);
```

15.2.4 Polyhedron

```
polyhedron(
    points,       // array of three-dimensional vectors representing a point set

    faces,        // array of four-dimensional vectors with each vector
                  // a surface tile whose edge points are given as indices into
                  // the points array

    convexity     // Optimization parameters for preview. If you experience
                  // rendering errors in preview, increase this value. A value
                  // of 10 should work in most cases.
);
```

15.2.5 Import of Geometries

```
import(
    file,         // filename of a `.stl`, `.off`, `.amf` or `.3mf`-file

    convexity     // Optimization parameters for preview. If you experience
                  // rendering errors in preview, increase this value. A value
                  // of 10 should work in most cases.
);
```

15.2.6 Surface from Image Data

```
surface(
    file,         // filename of a `.png`-file or text file

    center,       // if "true", the generated object will be centered

    invert,       // if "true", the color interpretation will be inverted

    convexity     // Optimization parameters for preview. If you experience
                  // rendering errors in preview, increase this value. A value
                  // of 10 should work in most cases.
);
```

15.3 Transformations

15.3.1 Linear Extrusion

```
linear_extrude(
    height,      // extrusion length

    center,      // if "true", the Extrusion will be centered along the Z-axis

    twist,       // twist in degrees around the Z-axis

    slices,      // number of layers along the Z-axis

    scale,       // Scaling of the base shape along the extrusion. Either a
                 // single value or a two-dimensional vector that defines the
                 // scaling in X- and Y-direction separately

    convexity    // Optimization parameters for preview. If you experience
                 // rendering errors in preview, increase this value. A value
                 // of 10 should work in most cases.
)
a_2D_geometry();
```

15.3.2 Rotational Extrusion

```
rotate_extrude(
    angle,       // angle of the extrusion around the Z-axis

    convexity    // Optimization parameters for preview. If you experience
                 // rendering errors in preview, increase this value. A value
                 // of 10 should work in most cases.
)
a_2D_geometry();
```

15.3.3 Translation

```
translate(
    v        // a two- or three-dimensional vector that describes the translation
             // relative to the origin
)
a_geometry();
```

15.3.4 Rotation

```
rotate(
    a,        // either a single rotation angle (in conjunction with v)
              // or a three-dimensional vector that describes the rotation
              // angles around the X-, Y-, and Z-axis

    v         // a three-dimensional vector that describes the rotational axis
)
a_geometry();
```

15.3.5 Scaling

```
scale(
    v         // a two- or three-dimensional vector that describes the scaling
              // of the geometry in X-, Y- and Z-direction
)
a_geometry();
```

15.3.6 Resizing

```
resize(
    newsize   // a two- or three-dimensional vector that describes the
              // new dimensions of the subsequent geometry. Values of 0 are
              // interpreted as "auto scale"
)
a_geometry();
```

15.3.7 Mirroring

```
resize(
    newsize   // a two- or three-dimensional vector that describes the
              // new dimensions of the subsequent geometry. Values of 0 are
              // interpreted as "auto scale"
)
a_geometry();
```

15.3.8   Color

```
color(
    c,        // either a four-dimensional vector that describes the color as
              // RGBA with values ranging from 0 to 1; or
              // a three-dimensional vector that describes the color as RGB with
              // values ranging from 0 to 1; or
              // a string that describes the color as hexadecimal code with a
              // leading '#'; or
              // a string that describes the color with a color name like "red"

    alpha     // a transparency value ranging from 0 (transparent) to 1 (opaque)
)
a_geometry();
```

15.3.9   Convex Hull

```
hull(){
    a_geometry();    // the convex hull is formed over all elements of the
                     // geometry set

    a_geometry();

    ...
}
```

15.3.10   Expansion and Shrinking

```
offset(
    r,          // expansion using a circle with radius r that is moved along
                // the 2D-shape. alternatively:

    delta,      // distance to the new outer shape from the original shape.
                // Compared to `r` sharp corners will not be rounded when using
                // delta.

    chamfer     // if "true", corners will be flattened (only in conjunction
                // with delta)
)
a_2D_geometry();
```

15.3.11 Minkowski-Sum

```
minkowski() {
    a_geometry();    // base geometry

    a_geometry();    // geometry that is copied at every point of the base
                     // geometry to expand the point set of the base geometry
}
```

15.3.12 Affine Transformation

```
multmatrix(
    m        // a 4x3 or 4x4 transformation matrix that describes the affine
             // transformation of the geometry
)
a_geometry();
```

15.4 Boolean Operations

15.4.1 Union

```
union(){
    a_geometry();    // all geometries of the geometry set will be united

    a_geometry();

    ...
}
```

15.4.2 Difference

```
difference(){
    a_geometry();    // base geometry

    a_geometry();    // all geometries after the base geometry will be
                     // subtracted from the base geometry

    ...
}
```

15.4.3 Intersection

```
intersection(){
    a_geometry();   // all geometries of the geometry set will be intersected

    a_geometry();

    ...
}
```

15.5 Loops

15.5.1 For-Loop

```
for ( i = [start : step : stop] )  // loop variable i goes from
a_geometry();                      // start to stop with increments of
                                   // step (optional)

for ( v = array )                  // loop variable v goes through all
a_geometry();                      // entries of the array

for ( i ... , j ... )              // multiple loop variables are separated
a_geometry();                      // by commas
```

15.5.2 For-Loop (Boolean Intersection)

```
intersection_for( ... )     // same operation as regular for-loop,
a_geometry();               // but objects are intersected instead of unified
```

15.5.3 Generative For-Loop

```
array = [ for (i = ...) i ];        // generates an array using a for-loop
```

15.6   Mathematical Functions

```
absolute value:        abs()
sign of a value:       sign()
```

```
sine:                  sin()
cosine:                cos()
tangent:               tan()
arcsine:               asin()
arccosine:             acos()
arctangent:            atan()
arctangent 2:          atan2()
```

```
round down:            floor()
round:                 round()
round up:              ceil()
```

```
natural logarithm:              ln()
base 10 logarithm:              log()
natural exponential function:   exp()
```

```
power function:        pow()
square root:           sqrt()
```

```
minimum:               min()
maximum:               max()
```

```
length of a vector:             norm()
cross product of two vectors:   cross()
```

15.7   Other Functions

```
number of elements in an array     len()
number of letters in a string      len()
concatenate arrays                 concat()
convert parameters into string     str()
search in arrays                   search()
character conversions              chr(), ord()
```

15.7.1 Local Definition of Variables

```
let (x = ...) {

}
```

15.7.2 Random Numbers

```
array = rands (
    min_value,      // smallest random value
    max_value,      // biggest random value
    value_count,    // number of random values
    seed_value      // random seed
)
```

15.7.3 Access to Outer Geometry Set

```
module test() {

    $children           // number of elements in the outer geometry set

    children( i );      // i-th Geometry of the outer geometry set.
                        // If no index is provided, all geometries of the
                        // geometry set are returned

}
```